The European Language Cl

Open Frontiers

Teaching English in an intercultural context

Wout de Jong

Heinemann English Language Teaching
A division of Reed Educational and Professional Publishing Ltd
Halley Court, Jordan Hill, Oxford OX2 8EJ

OXFORD MADRID FLORENCE ATHENS PARIS PRAGUE
SÃO PAULO MEXICO CITY CHICAGO PORTSMOUTH (NH)
TOKYO SINGAPORE KUALA LUMPUR MELBOURNE
AUCKLAND JOHANNESBURG IBADAN GABORONE

ISBN 0 435 24184 2

First published 1996

The author and publishers wish to thank the following who have kindly granted permission for the use of copyright material:

Addison Wesley Longman Ltd for an extract from *Present Day English for Foreign Students* by E F Candlin (1972); for an entry from *Longman Dictionary of Contemporary English*, Third Edition; for an extract from *Process and Experience in the Language Classroom* by Legutke, Candlin and Thomas (1991); and for extracts from *Language and Power* by Fairclough and Candlin (1989). Aitken & Stone Ltd on behalf of Paul Theroux for an extract from *The Mosquito Coast* (1983). Arrow Books Ltd (an imprint on Random House UK) for an extract from *A Case of Need* by Michael Crichton (1996). Cambridge University Press for extracts from *Discourse Strategies* by J J Gumperz (1982); from *Language and Linguistics* by John Lyons (1981); and from *Discourse Analysis for Language Teachers* by M McCarthy (1991). Harcourt Brace & Company for two extracts from *Introduction to Psychology*, Fifth Edition, by Ernest R Hilgard, Richard C Atkinson and Rita L Atkinson. Copyright © 1971 by the Publisher. HarperCollins Publishers for an extract from *Wild Swans* by Jung Chang, published by Flamingo (1991). Professor Geert Hofstede for six diagrams from his book *Cultures and Organizations: Software of the mind* (1991). Reprinted by permission of the author and copyright holder. L C G Malmberg BV for an extract from *Notting Hill Gate*, Textbook 1, by Huub Rutten and Frank van Ruysevelt (1986). Otava Publishing Company Ltd for an extract from *Challenge, English for Communication* by Anneli Luukas and Joan Nordlund (1994). Oxford University Press for an extract from *Success at First Certificate* by Robert O'Neill (1987); and an extract from *English Visa*, Student's Book 1 by Jon Blundell (1984). Penguin Books Ltd for an extract from *The Suffrage of Elvira* by V S Naipaul (1969). Prentice Hall Company UK for an extract from *The Language of Youth Subcultures* by S Widdicombe and R Wooflitt, published by Harvester Wheatsheaf (1995). Reed Books for an extract from *Origins: A Sceptic's Guide to the Creation of Life on Earth* by Robert Shapiro (1986); and an extract from *Among the Thugs* by B Buford (1992). Dr Philip Riley for an extract from his article 'Social Identity and Intercultural Communication' in *Levende Talen* (1989). The University of Chicago Press for an extract from *Cultural Misunderstandings* by Raymonde Carroll (1988). Ed Victor Ltd on behalf of Douglas Adams for an extract from *Mostly Harmless*, Copyright © Completely Unexpected Productions Ltd (1992). Houghton Mifflin Company for extracts from *The Corpse on the Dyke* by Janwillem van der Wetering, Copyright © 1976 by the author.

Whilst every effort has been made to locate the owners of copyright in some cases this has been unsuccessful. The publishers apologise for any infringement or failure to acknowledge original sources and shall be glad to include any necessary corrections in subsequent printings.

Cover photo by Moggy
Layout by eMC Design, Bromham, Bedford
Printed and bound in Great Britain by The Bath Press

For Toke, who helped me realize that honouring cultural difference is an important part of everyday living together.

Acknowledgements

The ideas which form the basis of the book have been discussed with so many people that it would be impossible to mention them all without being accused of omitting someone. On the whole I have learnt most from people I met at conferences, seminars, workshops, etc, organized by the International Association of Teachers of English as a Foreign Language, by the Dutch Association of Teachers of Living Languages (Vereniging van Leraren in Levende Talen), the Council of Europe workshops and conferences I was privileged to attend, a visit to the United States on the invitation of USIS and several visits to the UK, some of them sponsored by the British Council.

Some colleagues must be mentioned by name because of their direct or indirect contributions to the book. This is particularly true of Bryan Jenner, whose direct experience of more and less exotic cultures, including those of western Europe, have led to many an evening's chat on the topic of working abroad as a teacher of English, and Gerard Willems, whose European connections helped him and me never to lose sight of international and intercultural links in the training of teachers of English as a foreign language. Jeroen Gronheid helped hammer out the outline of the first version of this book, which was written for EFL students in training for phase one of secondary education in the Netherlands as part of a series on multicultural education. John Strange looked critically at my use of the English language in the first version, and stimulated my interest in the field of international contacts through stories of his experiences in eastern Europe. Arthur van Essen found so much to his liking in the first book that he felt it might be usefully reworked for teachers and students of EFL in the rest of Europe. Much of its present form I owe to his critical supervision and generous support. Finally, Jill Florent must be mentioned. She was instrumental in giving the book its present structure and content.

Wout de Jong

96 97 98 99 00 10 9 8 7 6 5 4 3 2 1

Contents

The author and series editor

Wout de Jong is a former Senior Lecturer in the English Department of Hogeschool Gelderland, Faculty of Education. He was involved in the drafting of objectives for foreign language teaching in the Netherlands for the first phase of secondary education, and was a member of the ATEE Working Group on the Education and Training of Language Teachers. He was one of the founding fathers of the Dutch Foundation for the Promotion of Language Learning and Teaching in the Netherlands. He was active in Council of Europe workshops for language teachers and teacher educators, and in many projects to do with improving foreign language teaching. He has published, both nationally and internationally, on these topics.

Arthur van Essen MA PhD is professor of Applied Linguistics at the University of Groningen in the Netherlands. He has been involved in EFL for the past 35 years as a teacher, a teacher trainer, and a writer of coursebooks. He has published widely and has lectured in Africa, the UK, and continental Europe. He was Vice-Chair of the International Association of Teachers of English as a Foreign Language (IATEFL) in the 1980s and the first elected Chair of Networking English Language Learning in Europe (NELLE). He is currently the Head of the Department of Language and Communication at the University of Groningen.

The European Language Classroom

EUROPEAN FOREIGN-LANGUAGE CLASSROOMS share a long tradition of language teaching and language learning. Most European nations are close to each other or they are bi- or multilingual themselves. The need to communicate with one another across languages is therefore an old and obvious one. Business is conducted in many European languages, and many Europeans spend their holidays in a neighbouring European country. Learning and teaching foreign languages is of enormous importance for Europe.

Traditionally, European foreign-language teachers share their learners' native language and culture. They have themselves been through the process of learning another language. As a result, they are themselves at least bilingual, but more often than not, multilingual. Such teachers tap a vast resource of both personal and collective experience. This is what sets the European language classroom apart from other language classrooms, whether native or second.

The European Language Classroom Series addresses issues that concern foreign-language teachers in both public and private-sector education. It aims to help you, the teacher or teacher trainer, to bridge the gap between current language teaching and learning theory and classroom practice, and to share and benefit from the expertise of foreign-language teachers who speak their pupils' mother tongue.

Individual titles in the series focus on: problems facing the novice teacher; developing classroom skills; intercultural learning and teaching; project learning; teaching a foreign language across the curriculum in state schools; managing change in teacher-training programmes; language for specific purposes; the psychology of foreign-language teaching; etc. In view of the rapid developments taking place in Europe the series is open-ended.

The authors share these concerns and have joined the team on the strength of the contribution they have made to foreign-language education, either in their own country or at European level. Authors will call on their readers to share their often considerable experience as teachers of at least one (and sometimes more than one) foreign language, and as learners of usually more than one foreign language.

Meeting the challenges posed by foreign-language teaching in a Europe in which all the barriers are lifted is what the European Language Classroom is about.

Arthur van Essen

Introduction

The history of the world is really the history of the people of western Europe. The history books pupils use at school take them through historical developments in the Middle East, Egypt, Greece and Ancient Rome and get into their proper stride when they arrive at the Middle Ages and the Renaissance. Then we arrive at a couple of centuries in which western Europe is fought over for political supremacy. The struggle is finally won by Great Britain through its use of sea power and the wealth it has accumulated from its colonies.

Now read this first paragraph again asking yourself if all your students/pupils would share this world view, particularly those originating from a variety of non-western countries. Their countries became involved in our concept of world history, but before they were confronted with our existence, people in these countries led their own lives, traded with neighbouring countries, went on expeditions, fought wars, wrote books, in short had a history and culture of their own. An interesting question is, whether they were happy to meet with representatives of our culture, and what they thought of them.

Up to the 1950s it was quite possible to live a happy life in one's own country without a thought for the outside world. In fact, there are quite a few people who insist that this is still possible.

Gradually, after the Second World War, most former colonies gained their independence. As a result of this, much of western Europe found itself confronted with its colonial past. The former colonies kicked out many people who had willingly served the colonial masters. More or less reluctantly they were accepted by the West. As long as their numbers were small, one could ignore their presence, but this happy state did not last very long.

These days it is no longer possible to act as if the natives of western Europe are still on their own. Particularly after guest-workers came to help out the labour force, western Europe has had to face facts. These days one can no longer get around having to accept that one's world view may not be shared by everybody else.

This book is intended to help practising and trainee teachers of English as a foreign language come to grips with the issue of multiculturalism. Some people might prefer to think that the easiest way out of the problem is to demand conformity to *their* standards in multicultural classes. Even if recent immigrants to western Europe are expected to adopt the prevailing system of norms and values, it is at the very least necessary for the natives to face alternatives to organizing society which have shown their value over a long time. Hence, what I have tried to achieve is a balance between the provision of facts and theories which may be helpful in the solution of problems, and activities which will, hopefully, lead to an open mind during the confrontation with other cultural norms and values.

The problem of intercultural education is something all foreign language teachers should consider, simply because language and culture are indivisible. It is not a revolutionary idea that there is a link between a culture and the language used by its members. Edward Sapir and Benjamin Lee Whorf claimed, in the early years of this century, that cultural background decides the way we look at the world around us. Whorf said: 'We dissect nature along lines laid down by our native languages.'

In its most extreme form the implication of the so-called Sapir–Whorf hypothesis is that mutual understanding of people from different language backgrounds is an impossibility.

Given that it is sometimes difficult enough to understand people who share one's own language and culture, I would still like to suggest that understanding other cultures may often be difficult, but never impossible. The main condition is that the people involved are willing to accept that alternatives to their own cultural values are possible and practicable. John Lyons puts this view slightly differently:

> **In short, it would seem that, despite assertions to the contrary by proponents of extreme determinism, no good reason has yet been found to jettison the more traditional view, that speakers of different languages have essentially the same world-view, or conceptual framework, as far as such deeper and philosophically more interesting topics as time, space, number, matter, etc, are concerned.**
>
> **It does not follow, however, that speakers of different languages have the same world-view in respect of other less basic concepts. For many of the concepts with which we operate are culture-bound, in the sense that they depend for their understanding upon socially transmitted knowledge, both practical and propositional, and vary considerably from culture to culture. (Lyons 1981 p308)**

It is certainly possible to study aspects of a cultural value system separately, but one day they have to be integrated into the larger whole. Learning a foreign language and thus becoming acquainted, to some extent, with a foreign culture may help towards relativizing one's own system of norms and values. The case for English may be somewhat different from other foreign languages, because it has become *the* international language. It is no longer an exotic language and the culture of its native speakers is not completely foreign.

EFL textbooks in Europe tend to concentrate on teaching and learning one model, British or American, of language and culture, and rarely take into account that English has become the international lingua franca with all that this may involve in intercultural confrontation. Most students and secondary school pupils are well aware of the status of English in international contacts, and usually manage to keep the things they are expected to do in school separate from life outside the classroom. Therefore the damage done by traditional approaches to EFL may not be lasting. Nevertheless, if the learning of EFL is to prepare learners for using language in intercultural contacts, the kind of learning envisaged in this book has to take place.

Although some cultural environments will find it very difficult to accept that there are no final, definitive answers to many of the issues raised in the book, a majority of teachers these days are agreed that learning is an activity of learners, and that teachers may help overcome difficult stages, may organize learning activities and try to stimulate the process, but can never predict the outcome.

It is my wish that this book will contribute to the furthering of mutual understanding and respect for cultural differences. If these do not come about, the chances for a European Union in which every person, young and old, male and female, can live a happy life, are slim.

How to use this book

It is the aim of this book to suggest ways in which (the training of) foreign language teachers may help learners to cope with contacts with other cultures. The problem is urgent, because the other culture is around the corner from where we live, quite literally for many people living in inner cities.

The book may be used for private study or as a coursebook in a study course on the multicultural classroom. It provides reading interspersed with *Activities*. These activities can be done privately, if one feels so inclined. Most are intended to raise the reader's awareness of one or other issue connected with *the learning and teaching of language and culture*. Where this seemed helpful some further information has been provided in a note at the end of the chapter.

If done as part of a course I would suggest that trainee teachers carry out the activity concerned individually, then compare notes and, if necessary, come to an agreement in small groups (three to five participants) and subsequently discuss the issue in class. In some cases it may be found helpful to rearrange small groups and allow time for discussion in these reconstituted groups, before the whole class compares group findings.

Chapter 1 Culture and language in an international world

The villagers had watched in consternation as the woman had marched boldly to the hut of the Sandwich Maker. The Sandwich Maker had been sent to them by Almighty Bob in a burning fiery chariot. This, at least, was what Thrashbarg said, and Thrashbarg was the authority on these things. So, at least, Thrashbarg claimed, and Thrashbarg was ... and so on and so on. It was hardly worth arguing about.
(Douglas Adams, *Mostly Harmless*, Pan Books 1993, p113)

Introduction

The first contact with another culture is fraught with many difficulties and dangers; some we may sense at once, and others we may only realize after a long time. For many people, particularly those born in western Europe and North America, the confrontation is dreadfully simple: 'You wade right in and tell those people what you think!' The scene described by Douglas Adams above illustrates, in a slightly exaggerated manner, the approach many western Europeans adopt when confronted with an unfamiliar setting.

It takes time for people to realize that perhaps the direct approach may not always work. The number of international incidents where it didn't work as expected are numerous: UN intervention in Somalia in 1992; in the former Yugoslavia in the same year; in central Africa in Burundi and Rwanda in 1994 and 1995; in Haiti in 1994, etc. Such incidents occur not only at the level of government, but also at the level of business companies and individual meetings with representatives of other cultures. What the consequences will be is not always clear, particularly at a personal level, but irritation is the least, followed by any reaction within the power of the people whose rights of privacy were so crudely invaded.

In this chapter an attempt will be made to define 'internationalization' (in the sense of 'meeting of two or more cultures'): history shows us that international contacts have always taken place. Recent increases in their number have a bearing on present-day developments, both socially and individually. This has important implications for teaching and learning languages for international communication. To come to a better understanding of the concepts of language and culture, we focus on the way language reflects culture. The notion of error, as this occurs in foreign language communication, will receive some attention. In this chapter the discussion will be relatively superficial, necessarily. In following chapters these issues will be tackled in more detail.

International contacts

The problems of meeting with another culture tend to be underestimated for many reasons. Since we, westerners, are members of 'powerful' communities, they, 'foreigners', look up to us. Also, we know about 'them', thanks to the blessings of international media communication. Switching on our TV set we know that we can watch programmes broadcast in most countries on the European continent, Great Britain or even America, and vice versa. The world we live in has become a very small one. We are able to see the world at home and at play and we take it all in our stride. We have become internationalists, true world citizens, living in a global village, switching from one culture to the other without any apparent difficulty.

This view is only partly true. The present technical facilities in the field of communication do make it possible for us to observe other cultures through the medium of documentary film or news broadcasts, radio and books. But the TV programmes most people watch are mainly those provided by their 'national' broadcasting services. Programmes, or parts of them, as for example in news items, will in most countries rarely be broadcast in the original language. They will have been translated, and then dubbed, ie an actor's voice takes over from the original speaker, or subtitled, ie presented in one or two words on the screen. Occasionally, if one's English is up to it, CNN or another English language satellite broadcasting station will be watched. And on the continent of Europe there are always the TV stations of a neighbouring country. But how many non-native people do actually watch these? And, if they do, do they really catch all the meanings of what they are watching? This of course depends largely upon knowledge of the other culture and the other language. On the whole one's knowledge of the world is perhaps sufficient to catch the main message. Occasionally one may have a problem understanding a particular broadcast.

Particularly in western Europe package holidays have brought foreign holidays within the reach of families on average incomes. Spain, France and Greece, to name a few, are flooded with holiday-makers from many countries during the summer. Not that this automatically means that every one of them will take part in the activities of the foreign community they happen to have landed in for the moment. Mostly the reverse is true, but some sort of contact does take place. The main obstacle in the way of establishing contact is often insufficient command of the foreign language on the part of the visitor. The natives may have a little English, and if the same is true of the tourist, it may be possible to establish a very narrow basis for mutual communication.

This becomes a different matter when people take a more active part in everyday life in another country, that is, when they come into daily contact with people and things foreign. They may have some experience of the foreign culture derived from holidays, they may know the language reasonably well, enough to be an observer, but becoming part of another social structure is a different matter. In fact, many popular holiday countries are quite familiar with the phenomenon of 'foreign' enclaves, areas which have been completely taken over by a group of German, Dutch or English people, mostly old-age pensioners who have invested in a holiday home abroad to spend the rest of their lives in a pleasant climate. Such people may have very little contact with the local population, and if they do, they are often completely surprised that their presence sometimes leads to local friction, or worse.

A problem in many respects comparable to the issue presented in the last paragraph is its opposite: the local ghetto mainly populated by immigrants attracted by the possibility of earning an attractive income abroad and then returning, 'rich' by the standards of their home country, to their native land. Such immigrants often find it difficult to be accepted by their new 'neighbours' because they take away job opportunities and housing from some members of the local population, while at the same time their customary habits of eating and drinking and their social contacts with fellow-countrymen create irritation and nuisance. In many European countries, and in the rest of the world as well, of course, problems of this kind cry out for a solution. Easy solutions are not readily available, but there may be a chance in attempts at widening people's horizons; in helping people to acquire an international outlook.

Activity 1.1 If you were in a position to advise on measures to prevent problems occurring between a group of foreigners, as described above, coming to live in your community, and the local population, what would you advise?[1]

Internationalization: historical trends

Many European countries have always had an eye for the international scene. The Dutch sailed all over the world conveying goods from one place to another. So did the British. The Swiss and the Germans supplied manpower, ie professional soldiers, to a great many European countries at one time, to fight their wars. Scandinavians went out to hunt and fish, but also established themselves in the US as immigrants. So did many Italians, Poles and Russians. The Spaniards and Portuguese colonized South America. Even Germany, once it had decided to reunite the Holy Roman Empire under one Emperor, joined the race to Africa to establish a few colonies there.

From *c* 1500 AD onwards western Europe managed to establish contacts in a large number of countries, even in closed communities like Japan. The contacting people might show a certain amount of willingness to pick up a working knowledge of the language spoken in the country concerned or else they imposed their own language on the foreign community, ie English if the contact originated with Britain, or Dutch, or French, or whichever other language was native to the contacting group. The decision depended on the relationship finally established with the country contacted. If the country was occupied and became a colony, the language of the colonial administration was the invaders' language. If contacts remained at the level of trade, the native language was respected and the outsiders, some of them at any rate, had to learn the other language.

In actual fact only a very small proportion of any country's population went abroad, and the number of (non-native) people who did learn to communicate in an exotic language, such as Japanese, was negligible. Learning another European language for purposes other than trade was relatively rare: it was certainly mainly an upper-class activity. People in the diplomatic service, in accord with the increasing French influence in Europe and the world, had to learn French, as today they need English. Those with a cultural interest generally managed to pick up some French or German or English, depending on their mother tongue, to cater for an interest in literature, music or art generally. The number of people with a similar interest in learning Spanish, Italian or one of the Scandinavian or Eastern European languages in addition to their own language was much smaller. At the same time contacts across the borders between countries have always taken place.

In fact, communication problems in border areas hardly exist, since the dialect in the area is virtually the same. A (Dutch) student once told me that he had always thought that John Wayne was a German actor, until he happened to watch him in a film which had not been dubbed for TV. The explanation was that this student used to live close to the German border and watched a serial, in which John Wayne had the main part, on German TV. For him the language spoken at home hardly differed from the German or Dutch he was exposed to by the media.

Activity 1.2 Which foreign languages did you study at secondary school? Why did you study these languages (or this language) and not others? Were your reasons for taking the foreign language(s) any different from the general aims stated above? Check among colleagues or fellow students whether their aims were different.[2]

Wars cause people to move

Most European countries have suffered from wars over the last two centuries, and earlier. After the Napoleonic wars of the early nineteenth century there was a relatively long period of internal political conflict in many countries, eg Italy, Germany. Around the 1850s a period of relative quiet set in. Then the struggle for supremacy on the European continent between Germany and France got going in the 1880s, while Russia focused on its eastern territories.

The world wars of the twentieth century seem to have put an end to political instability in most of western Europe. In spite of the wars the population remained fairly stable. The history books give the impression that wars are about political concerns and hardly affect local populations, although they had to supply manpower for the army, of course. Approaching armies have always caused people to flee from their homes. Many of them never returned after the fighting was over, having established themselves in the new community and not really feeling the need to return to their native land. A recent example occurred in the 1950s when many Hungarians fled to the free world before the Russian army, and another in the 1990s when many people were trying to leave the turmoil in the former Yugoslavia. Flight from approaching armies still causes people to leave their homes and find somewhere else to live, to judge from news reports from many places in the world.

Wars are mainly caused by what in German is called *die Wille zur Macht* (the lust to obtain more power). Historians generally bring forward 'economic motives' for the occurrence of war. This may be true at an abstract level, but quite often it is the mutual dislike between powerful people, representing their nations, which makes it impossible to come to an understanding. There may well be a relationship between a country's leader's 'lust for power' and the way a country deals with disputes with its neighbours, particularly when the dispute involves a small country and a big one. History abounds in wars fought between a big nation and a recalcitrant, small, neighbouring country. Sometimes such wars had surprising outcomes, but generally they ended with a re-drawing of the borders between the two, or the small country being incorporated into the big one. Occasionally a small number of battles on land or at sea led to a meeting at the conference table where the two countries, on terms of equality, tried to solve their disagreement. Quite often this sort of arrangement could only be made because both countries already shared a number of interests and thus the pressure to come to an agreement was stronger than the pressure to fight it out. Such a relationship between two countries was fairly unusual, as history books may show. Slowly, with the growth of democracy, it seems mutual respect also increases.

Activity 1.3 Relationships between neighbouring countries owe a great deal to 'accidents of history'. What stereotypes do your fellow countrymen cherish concerning the people living just across the borders? Assemble a list of such stereotypes. Is it possible to account for them on the basis of one or other historic event?[3]

Other reasons for moving

Another impression given by many history books is that the average person prefers to stay at home, learn a trade and spend most of their life in the community where they were born. Moving to another part of the native country is rare, let alone to another country. This impression is incorrect. Economic necessity is probably the main spur for people to leave the community where they were born.

Human beings are most adaptable creatures. There is no being on earth that has managed to establish itself so widely. (Shapiro 1986 has an interesting contribution to make on this point, as does Calvin 1986.) *Homo sapiens* originated in the tropics and now lives practically everywhere imaginable, in areas of extremes of cold and heat, in places where the sun hardly appears, where it is dry or wet all the time, high up in the mountains and deep down in the valleys, in coastal regions and in environments covered in ice and snow for most of the year. In short, if a particular place is not prone to very extreme heat, drought, cold or wet, humans have settled there.

Basically man's survival is due to two things: the ability to manipulate the environment, and fertility. The two are related in a fairly straightforward biological way. An area that produces an abundance of food will allow more creatures to enjoy the supply. Its population will keep on increasing until the moment the food supply dries up and a new balance must be found (cf. Calvin 1986 *passim*).

The industrial revolution is only one example of how man has affected his environment. It caused large numbers of people to leave their homes to find work and income that was not available in the local community. Starting in Great Britain it led to industrial revolutions in most parts of Europe with all that that involves for the environment, to mass migrations of working people to areas where there was work, to local population explosions, to rapid developments in communication networks, etc. Once a network of rail and waterways, and roads, was available to move the produce of agriculture and the products of industry from one place to another, it was only natural that people who could afford to would use these means of transport to find out what life was like on the other side of the hill.

Another incentive for many people in western Europe to move to a new environment offered itself in the context of colonization and trade, ie people moving from Europe to America, Asia and Africa.

It is only during the last forty years or so that the richer western European countries have offered 'work', in a context similar to the situation during the industrial revolution, to potential immigrants from a variety of southern European and Mediterranean countries. At the same time it has become easier for the average adventurous citizen to find work abroad, eg because a firm offers the opportunity.

In short, the number of people who live all their lives, from birth to death, in the same surroundings, is probably much smaller than the impression one is given. It was in this context that governments began to realize that social mobility across national boundaries might become a political issue. (See eg the publications of the

Council of Europe, particularly Council of Europe 1973 and 1989, dealing with topics in this area.)

Activity 1.4 Decide, from the surnames of people you know, whether their families originated from another country. Having established this, it may be possible to find out whether the move was from political, economic or other motives, eg if the time of their arrival can be worked out.[4]

Population pressure: another reason to move

It is only recently that we have managed the trick of not having as many children as we can. But we can afford this luxury only because we have learned to control many of the killer-diseases we used to suffer from in the past. It has taken us several decades to accept that it is no longer necessary to have ten to fifteen children to survive as a family. Developing countries are at present facing the problem of coping with a population which is increasing dramatically thanks to improved medical care, while the economic infrastructure is not (yet?) capable of providing for so many people.

Western Europe and North America have led the way in developments in medical science which have to a large extent made it possible to prevent disease. They have also introduced reliable forms of birth control, at least more reliable than before. However, before people accepted these new developments, the population of western Europe had increased – the post-war 'baby boom' – to such an extent that science had to come up with new ways of producing food to feed the masses, and ways of dealing with the resulting changes in the economic structure of society. These took time to come about and they affected the structure of society in the countries of western Europe, as a glance into any history book dealing with the last two or three centuries will show.

Developments leading to greater prosperity have always resulted in an increase in the number of people in the 'rich' environment. Parents succeeded in having more healthy children, and more of them stayed alive longer. Also, the prosperous area attracted people from elsewhere. Of course, as soon as local prosperity runs out, many people will leave for other parts of the country or the world where new opportunities offer. Thus, the baby boom after the second world war gave rise to large waves of emigration from western Europe to the United States, Canada, Australia and New Zealand.

Such demographic changes as many countries have experienced in the last three or four decades have always been part of the human experience, but perhaps not on such a massive scale as at present. These, particularly in areas where different cultures meet, may cause communication problems, which in their turn may cause friction and aggression.

Coping with other cultures

Once they have found their niche, people, ie those who have found a job, somewhere to live and living conditions to their liking, generally prefer to have things stay as they are. This is probably true of most people, wherever they find themselves on the social scale. The younger they are, the more willing people are to be adventurous, to go abroad, to make contact with other cultures, particularly when accepting that the challenge may bring in a pleasant income.

In European frontier areas the situation is different, and always has been. As long as the countries on either side are at peace, people cross the frontier: to find work, to go shopping, to visit local markets, or for a variety of other purposes. Communication is generally no problem: the dialect on either side of the frontier is usually virtually the same. As long as you speak the dialect, there are few problems. Such contacts have always existed along 'open' borders. In fact, family ties may have been present for many generations on either side of the frontier. But this 'local' situation is not generally shared by the rest of the population of the countries sharing a frontier.

Nowadays the number of pupils in primary and secondary education and of students in tertiary going abroad for a shorter or longer period of study is steadily increasing (cf. Bergentoft 1987 and 1989). In most instances such contacts are stimulated by the government of the country and sponsored by one or other European action programme. In short, the number of contacts between representatives of different cultures is increasing, developing into friendships and, in some cases, into marriages.

It is a rare person who does not need to learn to cope with the problems and questions this situation gives rise to. The provision of facilities to help students deal with 'culture shock' differ from country to country, but the need was recognized by the ministers of education of the European Union many years ago. Sub-network No. 9 of the *Reseau des Instituts de Formation* (RIF) is working hard at developing a definition of the European Dimension in Education within the context of the communicative approach to foreign language teaching. The teacher trainers taking part in and contributing to Sub-network No. 9 are convinced that foreign language learning and teaching has a unique role to play in achieving European citizenship, as languages are at the heart of our cultural identities. If we want to penetrate into what unites the European peoples and what distinguishes them from each other, we have to look at the way they communicate. As Europeans we also have to communicate cross-culturally and cross-nationally (see Willems 1994, pi, and 1995, *passim*).

I shall return later to the question of how individuals might cope with internationalization. For now let us have a further look at the situation as it presents itself today.

Internationalization: the present

There was a time when the population of any European country was uniformly white. The upper classes probably spoke a variety of the local language that virtually everybody else looked up to and held as the norm for acceptable language use. The present, in many western European communities, is completely different. A shopping trip to the local supermarket, particularly in many west European cities, proves the point: we are a multicultural, if not multiracial, society.

Activity 1.5 Go to the local supermarket, shopping centre, or town centre (outside the holiday season) for an hour and estimate the proportion of people coming from your own country, other European countries, African and Asian backgrounds.[5]

For many of our fellow countrymen the presence of people originating from other countries presents a threat to their everyday existence. The neighbourhood changes, particularly in the older quarters, where living is cheaper. For many indigenous people job opportunities fade; housing becomes problematic; local meeting points have to be shared with outsiders; change is forced upon them, which makes life much more problematic than it already is. This is mainly true of working-class areas, as it is mostly unskilled work that immigrants tend to be offered. Research in Germany, the United States and recently in Belgium indicates that the national economy profits to a very large extent from the presence of immigrants. The indigenous people must learn to live with them, and education can play an important role in helping the community, at all levels, to accept their contribution.

For a variety of political and economic reasons people may have left their native country and come to any country that would accept them. They may, for example, have moved of their own accord to fulfil a work contract in industry or commerce. They may be trying to escape persecution and discrimination in their home country or wish to escape poverty. If these people, as is the case with so many of them, do not or cannot return to their home countries, in due course the host country will have to solve several problems. Apart from all the immediate physical problems, such as the provision of food, medical services and accommodation, there is the problem of having to teach foreigners the language; they will have to learn to cope with another way of dealing with certain everyday occurrences, and the 'natives' have to accept these newcomers as members of the local community, and perhaps even of the family, not necessarily in that order, of course.

Internationalization and the individual

Anyone who has ever taken a pet into a completely new environment, for example when moving into another house, will have noticed how the new setting excites the animal, while at the same time making it very nervous. On the one hand a dog or cat is very curious to find out as quickly as possible what the new place is like. On the other it takes nothing for granted, returning again and again to the same spot to check whether anything is different from the last time. The turmoil lasts until it has become sufficiently familiar with the new surroundings to trust them.

This, in a sense, is the condition in which human beings find themselves, when confronted with a new environment. People, as well as pets, react in many predictable ways. They too, as it were, sniff around until they have made themselves familiar with enough living space. This may be the house and garden, if there is any, the street they live in and enough of the neighbourhood to know the way to the nearest shops. Gradually they will discover more: the way to the station, the school, the library, the cinema, the pub, the house of a friend, and so on. In due course they will feel sufficiently familiar with the town they have come to live in to stop exploring further. Enough 'safe space' has been created for their purposes and they feel no need to extend their 'territory'. This situation may remain stable for the rest of a person's stay in this particular area.

Any change in a person's familiar environment is cause for uncertainty, for fear, for suspicion, for aggression, in short any form of defensive action that will either remove the threat to a person's peace of mind or neutralize it. Alternatively, if the unfamiliar setting does not appear to be too threatening, one may become inquisitive and wish to find out more about the new environment. But, as the saying goes: 'curiosity killed the cat', warning us that we may be curious, but with caution.

Activity 1.6 Make a list of all the things that were different, that you found threatening, when you moved to the place where you live at present. (If you have not moved recently, imagine what you would have to cope with, when your familiar surroundings suddenly change because of an influx of a large number of political refugees.) Then decide which caused the most anxiety beforehand, and which in fact turned out to have been the biggest problem.[6]

These states of mind are, of course, extremes of a continuum of possible reactions to newness. Perhaps one that occurs most is the 'ignore all change' type of reaction, where people behave as if everything has stayed as it was, when anyone can point out things that are different. At the other end we find the reaction that insists on remaking the environment in the speaker's image.

Activity 1.7 In 1899 Earl Grey remarked:

> **Probably everyone would agree that an Englishman would be right in considering his way of looking at the world and at life better than that of the Maori or the Hottentot, and no one will object in the abstract to England doing her best to impose her better and higher view on these savages ... Can there be any doubt that the white man must, and will, impose his superior civilization on the coloured races?**
> **(quoted in Phillipson 1992 p45)**

What arguments would you use to refute the point of view expressed here?[7]

Opening the mind

Obviously, if people are willing to recognize that changes in the environment are 'normal', it would make it much easier to develop a state of mind receptive to change. This may not be part of one's social and cultural background and may therefore be difficult to acquire, but awareness of a problem goes a long way towards solving it. Developing an open mind to the ways of other cultures is a prerequisite to understanding people from other nationalities. Getting rid of stereotypes is part of the process.

There are many ways of dealing with the environment. The discovery that others deal with a familiar problem differently from the way you deal with it can be disturbing and exciting at the same time. Acceptance of this state of mind is necessary in developing tolerance and respect for different approaches to the world, the environment, in short to life in general. For many people, for example, the discovery that in other countries different rules apply to the consumption of food is hard to accept. Popular holiday resorts often try to solve this problem by offering facilities similar to the ones people are familiar with at home. In this way the local population will at the same time not be overly irritated by the presence of 'invaders'.

This type of 'escapist' solution to a problem is in the long term unacceptable in the context of living in our 'global village'. Everyone will have to face up to what the implications are of meeting representatives of other cultures. The acceptance of cultural differences depends in the end on the willingness of individual people to accept their approach to life as valid. The problem for education is that teachers cannot force their learners into acceptance: they can only present alternative ways of coping with life. For the people who are confronted with an influx of foreigners into their neighbourhood the solution is not so simple. Political decision makers will have to see to it that the change is not sudden but gradual.

Activity 1.8 Make a list of the changes to your way of life you had to cope with, when suddenly you became personally responsible for organizing it (either as a student coming to live away from home, or as a teacher in your first job). Is it possible to account for the changes? What about the things that stayed the same? If possible, compare your list to a similar list of a friend, male or female, who shares your background, and one who has a different cultural basis.[8]

Achieving mutual understanding

Communication has to work in at least two directions. In contact with a representative of another culture one cannot be certain of being understood in the way one wishes to be understood. The other's approach to the communication situation may involve the use of behavioural patterns that are unfamiliar to a person outside that social sphere. Depending on whether one belongs to a majority or a minority culture, reactions to such a situation are fairly predictable: the majority culture demands conformity to its standards, while the minority culture will hopefully try another tack. Neither type of reaction will necessarily lead to mutual understanding. It is therefore necessary to develop the skills which enable human beings to prevent communication problems.

A first step towards mutual understanding of representatives of different cultures consists in learning the other person's language. Obviously, the first priority for learning the other's language lies with the minority culture. At the same time those involved in looking after the welfare of migrants – social workers, doctors, nurses, etc – will need to be able to some extent to communicate in the migrant's language.

Activity 1.9 Draw up a questionnaire asking people, both native and non-native, about their willingness to accept changes in their environment, using a 5-point scale to score the replies. Topics should include housing, education, services, facilities for preserving the home culture, and perhaps a few others that apply particularly to your situation. Compare the results for different groups of the population and, if possible, discuss your conclusions with others who have done similar research.[9]

The process of learning another language is a first step towards widening one's cultural horizon and integrating into a receiving culture, if necessary. Hence the need for people whose native language is English to learn at least one other language.

The position of the English language as a lingua franca creates special difficulties in intercultural communication, particularly when both speakers use English as their second language. In following chapters I will discuss ways of overcoming these.

Internationalization and the collective

Acceptance of other cultures cannot be imposed by law. The law is generally defined as a codification of the rules of behaviour agreed on by society. The law in one country may thus be quite different from the law in another. Respect for the law is taught at home and at school. Another, related, function of education is the passing on of a country's cultural achievements to future generations. Much depends on what is understood by 'cultural achievements'. If in a particular country it is felt that tolerance for the opinions of others is part of its culture, this will be an advantage in the context of teaching a foreign language and its culture. But not every culture is open to alternatives. Openness to alternative cultures involves a willing reorientation as to the values held dear by the community one lives in. In this context it is a hopeful sign that the 1994 conference in Cairo on population growth managed to agree, to some extent at least, on measures that may help towards solving problems that will be caused by unlimited population expansion.

Parents and the school teach us 'attitudes and values'. Children often find it difficult to accept the demands of school in this respect, particularly when their parents' system of values differs from the system demanded at school. One of the problems a child and its parents may have to come to terms with is that the language used at home is unacceptable at school. This may be the local dialect, but also the 'home language' of parents who have emigrated to this new country. The consequences of not complying with the demands of the school are entirely predictable: isolation, discrimination and, depending on a number of factors, probably drop-out, drugs and/or a career in crime. The problem becomes worse in those parts of a town where the school mainly attracts children from a background where economic achievement is negligible.

Teachers working in such a setting and wishing to prevent their charges becoming involved in the drug scene and minor crimes find it extremely hard to protect those pupils who are ambitious and wish to improve their lot against the pressure to conform exerted by mates following their parents in condemning a society that does not give them a chance to earn a proper living. Such pressure is always present in social groups, although the amount of pressure may vary. The best solution to this problem seems to be for the local council to see to it that all schools receive a representative mix of children from all walks of life. This is the solution adopted in the US to overcome the problems created by 'black ghettos'.

Education is an important area, as are areas such as housing, employment and medical care. Does the government in your country arrange for schools which cater only for immigrant children? An interesting question is whether the children of immigrants should be taught their home language and culture at all. And if so, who should bear the cost of providing for 'home-language' teachers? And for what language communities should this provision be made available? Or should the children receive extra tuition to overcome possible handicaps caused by their background? Answers to these and related questions are not immediately available, unfortunately, but they have been widely discussed in the context of the work of the Council of Europe (eg Rey 1986).

Activity 1.10 Having to deal with a multicultural group may present many problems teachers may not always be aware of. Consider what ought to be done in such a setting (in fact, what you would do!), if confronted by some pupils making racist remarks, or discovering that some of your pupils are being bullied because of their race or religion or social background.[10]

Cultural achievement

Communities and countries are aware of their cultural achievements. They are passed on in various ways. Families often 'know' the contribution their members have made to the country's culture. At another level, people involved in neighbourhood social activities are entirely familiar with 'who did what' to achieve the present state of 'fame'. The history classes at school play a part, but historical fiction probably has a more lasting influence, and the same goes for historical films and TV serials. We are justly proud of our achievements and wish to defend them against intrusions from outsiders. Sometimes this may take rather drastic forms.

The 'establishment' in most countries has ways, and the means, to deal with threats to the *status quo*. A recent case is that of Salman Rushdie whose novel *The Satanic Verses* led Imam Khomeini to ban the book in Iran and demand the death of its author. The case of Aung Sangh Shi of Burma is comparable. The 'civilized' world has perhaps less drastic ways of dealing with threats to its established norms and values, but they are equally effective, as a little thought and reflection will undoubtedly reveal.

Awareness of the achievements of representatives of our culture – our heroes – is normal. It should perhaps be considered with a sense of their relative status. Heroes in one culture may well be looked upon as criminals or worse in another. An illustration is the behaviour of fans at (inter)national sports events. Police have to be present in force to prevent molestation of innocent bystanders on many occasions both at home and abroad. In a sense football fans are as aware of the historical achievements of their football club and as insistent on passing them on, as is the government that passes a law forbidding critical appraisal of its performance.

Activity 1.11 In a great many countries books have been forbidden at one time or another for a variety of reasons. At one time lay persons were not allowed to read the bible in countries that followed the Roman Catholic dogma. Can you think of two or three banned books in your country that are now part of the accepted literary canon? What change in social behaviour accounts for this?[11]

Cultural achievements of others

The presentation of other cultures in the school textbooks of a country is typical of the general attitude towards the acceptability of other behaviour within that country. Tolerance may not be a notable characteristic of a particular society. It shows in the attitude of governments and official bodies towards immigrants. Active measures may be taken to prevent the forming of ghettos, to teach all immigrants the language, to involve the women in emancipatory projects and much more, as opposed to a *laissez-faire* attitude in such matters.

National policy differs from one country to another making it difficult to tackle the immigration problem effectively. An explanation for the differences may be found in the urgency with which a country perceives the problem posed by immigration.

On the other hand there is also the way the country's policy-makers consider the need to 'sell' their cultural heritage to others.

Many countries have special funds set aside to spread their cultural achievements abroad. But sometimes surprising discoveries can be made in this respect. At the 1993 *Frankfurter Buchmesse* (Frankfurt Book Fair) the Dutch were invited to provide the main cultural exhibition. They did, in close co-operation with representatives from Flanders (the Dutch-speaking half of Belgium). However, it was not all that simple. When the original invitation was extended, the Dutch Minister of Culture had no funds available to finance this venture. It took the Dutch government a surprisingly long time to make up its mind, and it may well have been pressure from Flanders that finally convinced them that a Dutch contribution had to be made to the *Buchmesse*, to a large extent subsidized by the Dutch government. As a result of accepting the invitation many Dutch authors now find their work translated into other European languages and themselves invited to visit cultural events abroad.

Activity 1.12 Assuming that one day the European Union will lead to one autonomous 'European state', what will the culture of your country contribute to the culture of Europe? Make a list and, if possible, compare it with similar lists prepared by representatives from other European countries.[12]

Culture and language

One widely-used definition of language is: language is 'a means of communication'. This definition is only acceptable as far as it goes. It could well lead to undesirable misunderstandings, as language serves other functions as well.

Activity 1.13 In the context of language learning and teaching three terms are frequently used: mother tongue, language and dialect. Look up definitions of these in a number of dictionaries, including dictionaries of 25, or more, years ago. How have definitions changed, if they have?[13]

Other cultures usually define common concepts in more or less different ways from what we are used to. This, of course, may lead to learning problems when trying to master a foreign language, and to misunderstandings, if one does not realize that the other culture may observe different rules of 'good behaviour'. For example, the notion of 'family' to many people in western Europe comprises our next of kin: father, mother, brothers and sisters. At a pinch the grandparents are accepted within the circle, but they may start having problems with the inclusion of uncles and aunts; cousins are accepted only in exceptional circumstances. In English this distinction becomes clear in the use of *nephew* and *niece* alongside *cousin*. The children of brothers and sisters are accepted, but the children of uncles and aunts to a lesser extent. In southern Europe, and not only there, the concept of family covers many more people than in the north: cousins are certainly part of the concept of 'family'. The Dutch distinguish between *gezin*, meaning the unit of father, mother and children, and *familie*, meaning other relatives 'sharing a common ancestor'. The English word *family* is used in both senses.

Activity 1.14 Draw up a list of vocabulary, say ten words, where English has one word and your first language (or a language you know well, if English is your first language) uses two, or where English has two words and your language only one.[14]

Although it is convenient to use the above definition of 'language' (abbreviating it even to language = communication), the implicit suggestion that a new language can be learnt without reference to the way it handles various 'cultural' concepts is simplistic. Consider the case of a child that moved from one part of the country to another, perhaps a long distance away. In the new (linguistic) environment people may look upon things differently: assumptions about a long list of norms and values may no longer be true. In order to fit into the new community the child may have to readjust its use of language; not just pronunciation, but also choice of vocabulary and perhaps even of grammatical forms have to change. It takes time (days? weeks? months?) to come to terms with the new set of norms and values, but all children quickly adjust their behaviour to the demands of the new setting, keeping behavioural norms of the 'home' separate from the norms of the 'street'.

Young children on the whole adapt more quickly and completely than older ones, often renouncing the previous environment virtually completely. The amount of pressure to conform is perceptibly stronger the younger one is, becoming less towards the age of ten. The older one is at the time of moving house the less the pressure to accept the new setting lock, stock and barrel. A change in living conditions always involves changes in outlook on life, on relationships, on a variety of notions people normally take for granted.

Activity 1.15 Your neighbourhood has been designated as a reception area for people who have been allowed political asylum. You have been approached by representatives of the committee set up to see to their reception for a contribution to their 'schooling'. Since your background is 'languages', you have been asked to draw up a syllabus for learning to cope with your native language and culture, and to find suitable textbook materials. The time available for intensive work is ten days, and, after this initial period, two mornings or two afternoons a week for a year. If possible, compare your notes and suggestions with the solutions to the problem developed by others.[15]

Coping with a new language

People do not always adjust easily to new circumstances. The problem may arise that the demands of the new setting clash with the requirements of the old and familiar. For some this may create a problem of social uncertainty (cf. Christophersen 1973 pp80–1). Psychologists have long been familiar with this phenomenon, calling it *anomie*. The discovery that *anomie* could also occur in the foreign language classroom is fairly recent. To a certain extent learning another language does imply adopting other cultural norms and values in settings where the new language is 'dominant'. In the early 1970s Canadian researchers (Gardner and Lambert 1972) discovered that one of the reasons that some pupils were no longer motivated to learn English or French as a second language could be linked to the problem of having to adjust their conception of the world. Some pupils refused to do this, showing symptoms suspiciously close to the condition of *anomie*, and wanted to have nothing further to do with learning another language. One wonders how far perhaps parents played a role in the development of *anomie* in their children?

To a large extent, apparently, human beings identify with the culture they live in, using the language of this particular culture also to supply themselves with an identity. We are nobody, unless we are part of a linguistic community. This linguistic community is not necessarily identical with the language community. There are obvious overlaps between the two, but also important differences.

A linguistic community shares words and ideas, norms and values. This phenomenon occurs among the active members of a students' club, among language teachers, officials, and many more social/linguistic communities. The point is that people belonging to a group of professionals, or a sports club or other institution, like a Rotary Club, in short *any* organization which focuses their interests and concerns, will share a language which sets those belonging to the group apart from those who are outsiders (cf. Fairclough 1989). In this context, insiders tend to use *jargon*: language forms, which may be completely incomprehensible to outsiders. The use of *slang* also belongs in this category, except that slang is generally considered to reflect a low social status in its user. Jargon often implies that its user has attained high social status.

Activity 1.16 Make a list of words that are peculiar to a type of setting you are familiar with, like a youth club, a sports club, chess, computers, car maintenance, etc. Try to find at least one person with whom you can compare notes. If possible, the more people involved in the same 'field' of this activity the better.[16]

A linguistic community does not only share a code of language, it also shares a code of behaviour. This code of behaviour is ignored on pain of finding oneself an outsider. Many clashes between parents and children originate from differences between the system of norms and values at home and the one valid among their friends. Sometimes a code used in a specific group is copied into general usage, as in the case of neologisms.

French people, for example, shake hands on a great variety of occasions, when introducing themselves, when meeting again, when saying goodbye. This custom has spread widely. For most people on the continent shaking hands is an everyday occurrence, though perhaps not as often as in France. English people on the whole restrict 'shaking hands' to the moment of meeting someone for the first time. Consequently they find it very difficult to adjust to the continental code in this respect.

People adopt new behavioural practices because they wish to impress, wish to set a new trend, wish to show their adaptability, or simply wish to be different. The opposite also occurs. Particularly when a person perceives the amount of pressure to conform to specific rules of behaviour as too insistent, it is quite common to find such a person sporting non-conforming behaviour. This may explain why many immigrant parents from an Islamic background will insist on their daughters wearing the traditional head-dress, which perhaps in their country of origin is becoming unfashionable.

Language communities may consider certain topics taboo: they are not discussed unless the people involved know each other very well. In Britain, for example, one does not discuss one's income, which in the US is a safe topic of conversation. Similarly, it is often unsafe to discuss one's own or another's religious conviction in the Netherlands; in many parts of Britain this would hardly raise an eyebrow. Philip Riley tells the story of the foreign housewife, married to a Frenchman, who entertained a group of her husband's friends to a meal, and who left the dinner table in tears when the guests discussed what she had cooked, mentioning alternative ways of preparing the food. As it turned out her guests had broken a taboo of her home country, whereas discussing recipes in France is one way of showing appreciation of a well-prepared meal.

Activity 1.17 Have you personally, or has anyone you know, experienced a (multinational) setting where a member of the company committed a social misdemeanour that on reflection may have been caused by a difference in cultural background? Make a note of any such occurrence and establish the possible cultural rules which may have given rise to the behaviour leading to the 'mistake' committed.[17]

Stereotyping foreign behaviour

Prejudice is often reflected in the way we talk about, or refuse to talk about, certain topics. The way 'perfidious' and 'Albion' are generally associated in France reflects what many French people subconsciously feel about the British. Or, to take another example, when some time ago a racist incident in a large German town was widely reported in the Dutch press, one broadcasting company took it upon itself to organize a postcard protest. The German government received thousands of postcards from Dutch citizens insisting that they were: 'very angry that nothing was done about these neo-fascist incidents'!

Members of one culture cherish stereotypical views of members of other cultures. (An interesting source of stereotypical information about Europeans is Hill 1992, *We Europeans*.) The Dutch look upon the English as typically trustworthy, friendly, approachable people; they are almost like the Dutch themselves in many respects. The reputation of the Germans on the other hand is terrible: they are harsh, overbearing loudmouths who insist upon occupying their particular spot on the beach and everything that goes with it. The French are too far away to have much of a reputation, apart from the Latin-lover type of fame, but if they do have one, it is one of arrogance (according to a recent interview with the French Ambassador in *NRC-Handelsblad*). French cuisine and French wine enjoy a high reputation in the Netherlands, even among those who have never even seen a four-star restaurant from the outside. French is still the language of upper-class culture in many respects. Similar stereotypes exist in many countries about their neighbours and to a lesser extent about the inhabitants of countries somewhat farther away.

Activity 1.18 What is the reputation of the neighbouring cultures in your country? Do their languages figure in the school curriculum? Why and how should one try to overcome these stereotypical points of view?[18]

Being a member of one culture and sharing its language generally means sharing a set of pet beliefs, prejudices and aversions about those who speak other languages. This may also be true of people who may share our language but who are not members of our linguistic community and do not share our culture. Consider the case of the Dutchman fluent in English, but having a noticeable accent, who some years ago found himself accused of holding an 'apartheid' point of view in relations with coloured persons. Apparently, his pronunciation of English was associated with 'Suid-Afrikaans' and consequently all the associations with 'apartheid' came to the fore. Or take the German lady who has lived in the Netherlands for several years, and speaks Dutch, but with a slight accent. One day, going into a shop, she addresses an elderly gentleman and asks him for the way to a particular building. He sort of looks at her without expression. She repeats her question politely. He produces a funny sort of smile and says 'Say Scheveningen'. She refuses to react, but is completely unable to utter a word (Glade-Hasenmüller nd.). For most foreign people learning Dutch the phoneme /X/, as in the Scots pronunciation of *loch*, is notoriously difficult. In fact, it is one of the tongue-twisters Dutch people traditionally use to catch out foreigners. Speaking the same language is obviously not always a guarantee of mutual understanding.

Activity 1.19 Make a list of pet beliefs, prejudices, etc held by many of your fellow-countrymen about minority groups living in your country. Check this list with others, if possible. Then separate the pseudo-problems from the real ones and devise a policy for overcoming the prejudices.[19]

Language: reflection of culture

Learning norms and values is part of the language learning process. Children are constantly told not to do this, to stop doing that, and so on. They are also encouraged to do things that are allowed, of course. As part of the process they are told to avoid the use of certain words – swear words, for example – until this has become second nature in certain situations. We all know that – to come back to swearing – there are occasions and circumstances where it is perfectly acceptable to use bad language.

A culture is a unified belief system. We interact confidently and with few misunderstandings with others who share the system of rules of behaviour our culture has developed. We know when we can call a friend on the phone, or at what time it is appropriate to drop in for an informal visit, or what to expect when we consider someone a friend. But these rules are not immutable. Under the influence of friends, pop music, TV serials or perhaps things they read the younger generation will experiment and try out new 'rules' on their parents, teachers and other 'old' people they know. When this occurs, a common (senior citizen's) objection may well be: 'Well, that's all right for them. I expect a different kind of treatment when you are dealing with me!' Alternatively, the senior citizen may find the change acceptable, but may add the proviso: 'It's all right when we are together, but I expect different behaviour from you when X is present.' The cultural code of behaviour is not immutable, but it may take some time before changes have become obvious and generally accepted.

A language is, in many ways, a reflection of the culture that uses it. This is true of both language communities and linguistic communities. Fishing communities talk differently about their living conditions than farmers or city dwellers, simply because their living conditions are different. But the vocabulary and grammar they use is part of the code used by the language community. A family moving from a farming community to a fishing community will have to adapt itself to the language of the new linguistic community to some extent – the extent depending on the age of the newcomer – and perhaps change some of their ways of dealing with neighbours and friends.

Coming to terms with and opening minds to alternatives to their own value systems and codes of behaviour should become one of the objectives of education, particularly language education. Fortunately this realization finds expression in statements of language teaching objectives and aims in many countries (Byram *et al.* 1994). As language teachers it is not our brief to bring about cultural change; rather it is our task to help learners to understand that other people may have different standards of behaviour which do not make them live unhappier lives than most of us do. If this happens to lead to cultural change, perhaps so much the better. Indeed:

> **'Awareness' is not 'understanding'. It is not enough to know that there are other ways of seeing and experiencing the world, that there are other cultural identities. Learners need to know and experience that, from other people's point of view, *they* are the 'foreigners', *their* mode of thinking and acting seems unnatural. This is a far more significant purpose for language teaching than simply learning to 'get by' when on holiday or use the foreign language in a sales-pitch.**
> (Byram 1992)

Activity 1.20 You have made friends with someone whose background is different (his/her parents are first generation immigrants into your country). You have been invited to visit your friend's family for the weekend. What do you need to know about your friend's cultural background to avoid social misdemeanours while you are with them? Make a list of points you need to know about. If possible, find out the answers from 'your friend'.[20]

Learning culture

Many people think that learning a language is as simple as learning to distinguish between good and bad. It is much more. Learning a language also means learning when to use what to whom, when to avoid using the expression that was perfectly fitting when you used it before in a different context. Like the young shop assistant's: 'There you are, dear,' and the old lady reacting: 'Don't you "dear" me!' Learning a language, first or second language, involves learning the conditions that make it necessary to invent new ways of expressing things. Many language teachers still insist on learning words and grammar, whereas learning proper behaviour in another cultural environment should receive at least the same amount of attention.

It always amazes language students to hear about Eskimos having *seven* words for different types of snow. A little reflection makes it clear that an Eskimo's life may depend on identifying the exact conditions of the snow, when he has to go outside to find food. For us, living in a milder climate, 'snow' is snow and we can always determine whether its condition is about right for skiing or whether we had better wait another day. But all languages show similar phenomena. Humans invent new words when there is a need for them. How many different words does your language have for different types of 'home'? The Dutch language has at least eight: *huis, boerderij, villa, bungalow, woning, appartement, paleis, flat.*

Activity 1.21 Within the context of 'precipitation', how many English words for different kinds of stuff falling from the clouds can you think of? Do the words (always) correspond with words in your own language? If not, how does your language express the same idea? How many words does that take? Check with a dictionary if necessary.[21]

Human languages make up new words when they are necessary. The words are always available to describe what we are getting at – there is no real problem for us in describing seven kinds of snow – but that is a clumsy way of talking about something you have to deal with every day. So, you get around the problem by agreeing about the meaning of an invented word with the people who are in the same situation as you are. Or, you borrow a term from another language. Thus terms like *glaznost* and *perestroika* were adopted by many languages when the changes in the Soviet Union were hot news. Or, you adapt a term familiar from a similar context: like *Dianagate* to refer to the commotion surrounding an almost indecent photograph of Princess Diana working out in a sports centre, on the basis of *Watergate* which referred to an unsavoury episode in the Nixon era in the US. This is how new words may get into the language. If enough people find it useful to include the new word in their vocabulary, it stays. Of course, when the word is no longer useful, it disappears from usage.

Activity 1.22 New words come and go. Make a list of words in your own language that are common among your peers, but perhaps unfamiliar to your parents. (A good idea is to take a walk through the centre of the nearest big town and check in shop windows, and places where food and drinks are sold.) How many of these are derived from minority languages used in your country? What do they mean, ie refer to? Which of them will end up in generally accepted usage, do you think? What arguments can you think of to support your view?[22]

Learning a new code

Differences between languages show up in many areas. They are apparent in obvious places like vocabulary and grammar, but particularly in the area of language use called pragmatics. This shows in social behaviour, for example in politeness formulas, but also more generally in the way people see the world around them. Learning to cope with the differences between the language behaviour in your own language and the foreign language takes time and has its ups and downs.

A Dutch businessman having dealings with his partner from Spain or from Italy may be able to communicate in their language, but still find himself in difficulties. One area may be the following: the Dutch prefer to deal with business first before getting round to more social matters, which southern Europeans would rather do the other way round. If you are not aware of such rules of social behaviour you may commit serious mistakes and cause offence. It is not enough to have learnt the code; it is equally necessary to learn the behavioural – non-verbal – code of the language community, and, in the case of the Dutch businessman, of the specific language community he has dealings with.

An interesting area of research in this context is the problem of 'transfer', that is, the tendency to copy a particular feature of one's native language (and culture) and use it in the foreign language. Learners are usually warned against this tendency and are, usually quite rightly, suspicious of features in the foreign language which resemble features of their own. Eric Kellerman (1987), who studied this aspect of language learning in depth, discovered three stages of development. During the first, learners do not really bother about the 'acceptability' of a particular use of words which have a direct counterpart in their native language. In the second stage they tend to reject word combinations resembling phrases from their own language. And in the final phase they tend to 'know' the possible phrases and reject the unacceptable ones.

Activity 1.23 Make up a list of words and short phrases in English, some translations from your native language, others original English phrases resembling expressions in your language, eg: 'I wish to become a new shirt' (which is clear when one knows that German *bekommen* translates as *to receive* in English), or 'To keep an eye in the sail' (which translates literally into Dutch *een oogje in het zeil houden*). A collection of 'false friends' should offer some help. Find an occasion to offer these to your learners to decide the stage of development they have achieved so far in English.[23]

Languages in contact: (mis)communication

Even if you have studied another language for some considerable time, this does not always mean that you manage to avoid misunderstandings. Probably you will be more aware of possible traps, where you have learnt not to wade in confidently, and as a result avoid problems.

There is the case of the British University lecturer who has been working in France for many years. His French is more than adequate for coping with the problems of everyday living in a French city, though he speaks it with a noticeable accent. However, whenever French drivers stop to ask the way, it is a regular occurrence that they turn away from him and ask a native for directions (Philip Riley, personal communication). Apparently his pronunciation of French causes native speakers to think 'He doesn't speak proper French, a foreigner: he can't help me!'

There was the case of the Dutch teacher of English who wanted to phone a friend while on a visit in London. As he had lost his friend's telephone number he called Directory Inquiries from a public telephone. He was asked to supply the number of the phone he was calling from, and reacted, when he didn't find it quickly and tried to win time, by saying: 'I don't think that will be necessary ...'. But before he had finished the sentence, he was rewarded with a 'click' and communication was broken. The explanation must be that the Dutchman's English was too 'native-like'. 'He should know what the custom is in this setting, so ... I have no time to waste. Let him call again!'

Intonation is a well-known problem area. Gumperz (1982) gives the following example, discussed in Wong (1985):

> **Indian women, newly hired to work in a British airport cafeteria, were having problems with their supervisors and their customers, both of whom felt that the women were surly and unco-operative. The Indian women, for their part, were perplexed by the reactions that they were getting and consequently felt discriminated against. From the tape recordings of the interactions, Gumperz observed that when customers who had ordered meat were asked whether they wanted gravy, the Indian workers would say *gravy* with a falling intonation. (...), this would be heard by British speakers as 'This is gravy. Take it or leave it.' (...) It was only after their attention was called to the way British employees made the same offer by using a rising intonation (*gravy*?) that they could see the source of the problem.**

When addressed by a person who does not speak our language perfectly, we do accept that this person will make errors. But some mistakes are perhaps not recognized as such and may give rise to unwarranted character judgements. It is this unfortunate human characteristic, making snap judgements about people's characters on very slight evidence, that leads to stereotyping and worse. In fact, in many cultures dialect speakers find themselves on the receiving end of derogatory character judgements, simply because they do not speak according to the 'accepted (upper-class) norm'.

Activity 1.24 Make a recording of a number of people speaking English, both native and non-native speakers, and offer this recording to fellow trainees/colleagues, asking them to indicate their estimate of each of these people, using the following *personality scale*:

intelligent	1 2 3 4 5	unintelligent
of high social status	1 2 3 4 5	of low status
highly ambitious	1 2 3 4 5	unambitious
authoritative	1 2 3 4 5	no leader of men
self-confident	1 2 3 4 5	irresolute
careful	1 2 3 4 5	casual
reliable	1 2 3 4 5	unreliable
strong-willed	1 2 3 4 5	weak
interested	1 2 3 4 5	indifferent
friendly	1 2 3 4 5	inimical
warm-hearted	1 2 3 4 5	unsociable
spontaneous	1 2 3 4 5	reserved
cheerful	1 2 3 4 5	nagging
modest	1 2 3 4 5	arrogant

(derived from AJM van Erp, *The Phonetic Basis of Personality Ratings*, Voorburg: PPT Research 1991)[24]

Sometimes miscommunication occurs because of a 'misreading' of what someone actually means. The following dialogue illustrates what I mean:

TEACHER: A, would you like to read this passage aloud, please?
A: Er ... well, no, thank you very much.

A interpreted the teacher's words as a wish to know his preferences, whereas the teacher wanted action. (Philip Riley, personal communication)

Conclusion

Clearly, there are many ways in which communication can go wrong. Mostly it is not simply a matter of mispronouncing a word, although this may raise eyebrows, or of misusing a grammatical rule. Quite often, in fact, it is an advantage to be immediately recognizable as a foreigner. The problem really occurs when we are not aware that we have stood verbally on someone's toes. This happens perhaps more often than we realize when we try to use another language. The way out is not to make others use our language, because this only makes us more aware of how sensitive our toes are. The solution must be to learn other languages and become alert to how other cultures function, and accept their ways of behaviour as equally valid as our own.

Notes

1 This is a type of problem a local council may have to decide on when confronted with the request of a property developer who plans to build 'holiday homes' for the affluent. Obviously there are a number of advantages, mainly economic, to the developer, but also in due course to local tradespeople. One way of tackling this problem may be to discuss first of all, with a group of students, who will profit from the decision and in what way; then, what may be the reaction of the rest of the population. How can one avoid negative reactions from the group that is mainly 'indirectly' involved? The number of possibilities for laying down the 'law' are severely limited, unfortunately. Apart from a number of broad measures, aimed at 'increasing understanding and respect for the point of view of native inhabitants on the one hand and that of the foreigners on the other', 'creating a basis for mutual understanding' and 'aiming for a European citizenship', however necessary these are, probably the only way to avoid such problems is by establishing mutual contacts with the local population, which can really only be done through learning the local language and culture.

2 This activity is probably more suitable for students, dealing with it in groups, than for individuals. What will come out is probably that in some cultures study of languages is considered something done when and if necessary. English is fairly important for international communication, and the rest hardly deserves attention: in short, a narrow-minded point of view, but amazingly widely held. Some, mainly the smaller countries, may prescribe the learning of the main European languages, ie German and French alongside English. In many countries the learning of other languages is to a large extent left to girls; boys taking by preference the more 'exacting' subjects: maths, physics, etc.

3 Stereotypes are mostly negative, referring to characteristics not particularly appreciated in one's native country. When they concern related versions of the same language, like the English spoken by people from Ireland or the Dutch spoken by people from Flanders, expressions often refer to the intellectual capacities of the speakers concerned.

4 Sometimes the spelling of a name gives its origin away: *Stempleski* must be of central European origin. Dutch widely uses place names, preceded by *van* (cf. French *de*, German *von*, etc.): *van Essen*, thus, might indicate someone originally from the city of *Essen* in Germany. In the English language the prefixes *Mac-* or *Mc-* originally meant 'son of' and perhaps indicated a Scottish (*Mac-*) or Irish (*Mc-*) origin. Place names are not very prominent in family names.

5 It often comes as a shock to many people to discover that the percentage of foreigners living within the neighbourhood is so large. It is therefore a very useful activity to carry out with pupils and students, particularly when there have been murmurings of ultra-nationalistic feelings. Add to this as a follow-up a discussion of 'why these people have come'.

Note: The activity is mainly relevant in EU countries. The further east one goes the more difficult it will be to spot obvious 'foreigners', except perhaps in the holiday season.

6 Again an activity one might very usefully do with a class of pupils who generally trust each other. It is always amazing for the person who has lived in the same place all their life to discover how much anxiety and fear moving to another part of the country can bring about, particularly when the neighbourhood the family has moved into seems to indicate that they are not welcome. Alternatively, sudden changes in the familiar environment are also cause for many people for anxiety and fear.

7 Clearly any assumption of superiority must be based on something that you do better. Moral superiority can perhaps only be based on the fact that the society of which you are a member looks after its individual members better than any other. The discussion about these and related issues is endless, but very useful for students (and teachers!).

8 This is a very useful activity for students, particularly if they can compare their notes with the experience of older people (the teacher?). A useful follow-up is a discussion about the amount of 'preparation' individuals received from parents, other members of the family, friends who had already made the change, etc. This activity may also be used as an introduction to figuring out what foreigners coming to live in 'our' country may have to cope with, and what sort of help and guidance might be supplied.

9 A possible helpful approach to developing the questionnaire might be to discuss the issue with a group of students, or colleagues, particularly if a multicultural setting is available. First of all discuss with them what topics should be included. Here the list from the previous activity might be helpful. Then draw up the questions and discuss who should try and get replies in what part of the town or neighbourhood.

10 There are no simple solutions to dealing with this kind of situation. One approach is to take the offenders aside and tell them that you have heard, promising punishment in the case of future

misconduct. Perhaps a better approach, particularly with a view to results, is to play the innocent and start a discussion on 'differences' and 'individuality', using any personality description that happens to be available as a starting point to a discussion of the question: 'Why should everybody behave in the same way?' (ie 'like you?')

11 Obscenity was quite often the excuse for banning a book. Generally, of course, the book in question went into matters that the ruling class felt it would be better to keep under cover. This happened to titles which since have become part of the literary canon: Dante's *Divina Commedia*, Boccaccio's *Decamerone*, Miguel de Cervantes' *Don Quijote*, James Joyce's *Ulysses*, DH Lawrence's *Lady Chatterley's Lover*, Jean Paul Sartre's *La Nausée*, and many, many others.

12 Professor Louk Hagendoorn of the University of Utrecht has carried out research into the field of national characteristics and stereotypes. His findings lead to the conclusion that national characteristics, although they are attributed by outsiders, are basically non-existent, ie certain individuals do show them whereas other members of the same nation do not (Hagendoorn and Linssen, 'Nationale karakteristieken en stereotypen', Universiteit Utrecht, Algemene Sociale Wetenschappen, Postbus 80140, 3508 TC Utrecht, photocopy 1991). On the other hand contributions in the field of the arts are probably readily available.

13 'Dialect' in my country used to have a 'bad' connotation. I assume that this is true of other countries. If so, it might clear up some of the fog in your trainees' (and teachers') minds to discuss with them the cultural basis of such ideas. The 'language' found in school textbooks is derived from 'accepted usage', ie accepted by people in the upper echelons of society.

14 This activity can be very usefully done in pairs. Useful sources of information may be available in collections of 'false friends'. The activity will bring out areas of everyday life that are similar and different in the two cultures. A bilingual dictionary is clearly a necessary support for this activity. Also, students will find this activity confusing, particularly where they have been taught that there is a one-to-one relationship between words in one language and another.

15 The main aim of the syllabus must clearly be 'survival' in the new environment. Much time should be set aside for becoming acquainted with 'everyday living' as organized in your culture. Simple things like: What does it mean when someone invites you for a coffee? At what time of day are you expected to turn up? Are you expected to bring a present for the host? If so, what kind? The language content might be more concerned with 'coping' than with 'grammatically correct utterances'. Attention should be given to things like going shopping, asking for information, directions, etc, making a person's acquaintance, going to the doctor. In the materials there should be sufficient space set aside for 'organizing a dialogue' (does this obey similar rules in both cultures?), 'who starts a conversation?', and 'when/how can the learner do this?' Consult, when in doubt, the guidelines available for this kind of work in your country, which will probably be based on similar work done for the Council of Europe in the context of describing basic levels of language command for the languages of its member states.

16 If this activity is done with a group of trainees, it may be helpful to organize the group around a number of topics agreed beforehand. The aim is to make individuals realize how many foreign (often English) words have entered everyday language use in areas of language use they are familiar with. The realization that Great Britain and the US have led the world in many areas of work and spare-time activities may sometimes be helpful in discovering that humanity cannot really survive on the basis of individuality, but needs to co-operate in most areas of living.

17 There are long lists of anecdotal information on this topic. Chapters 2 and 3 will deal with the issue in more detail. One such anecdote will have to suffice. There was an English student staying at a Dutch university for a year. He had picked up a little Dutch and, since most Dutch people are reasonably fluent in English, he had few problems. One day he went shopping and went into the local baker's. There were a few people present. One of the ladies behind the counter finished serving a client and said: 'Wie kan ik helpen?' (literally: 'Who can I serve?'). The young man stepped forward, saying: 'Mij' ('me'), to the consternation of the clients in the shop waiting their turn.
What went wrong was of course that the English student 'read' the invitation wrongly. In the Netherlands this is a quite common, indirect, polite way of asking whose turn it is. But see also note 20.

18 See notes 12 and 17 for more information. The issue is, of course, that one learns a language because one wishes/expects to have to communicate with its native speakers and others who use the language as a lingua franca. Cherishing stereotypes about the inhabitants of neighbouring countries will not help towards mutual understanding. Talking about such topics may help to start some people thinking. See also note 19.

19 On Dutch TV recently there was presented a series of four programmes for young viewers, a co-production, dealing with prejudices against the Germans. The 'adult' makers of the programmes found that the Dutch held many more negative views about the Germans than the other way round, and also that those young Dutch singers, footballers, etc who are making a career in Germany have very quickly got rid of their pet beliefs. Apparently experiencing the 'real thing' is the best road towards solving the problem.

20 It is amazing how much can go wrong by relying on one's own cultural norms. Consider the case of this Dutchman invited to dinner with a South Korean colleague. All was extremely pleasant, the food was superb, when suddenly the Dutchman noticed that his host and his wife left the table, then his host returned, and after about 15 minutes the hostess came back with a fresh helping of the main course, for him! It turned out that his hosts had the impression that he was still hungry after a number of helpings, which he wasn't. The Dutchman had been betrayed by his cultural norms. He had, without thinking, emptied his plate after each helping, which his hosts read as: he wants more. (Dr S Hylarides, personal communication) The conclusion must be that one needs to know as much as can be assembled about everyday behaviour, politeness formulas, times at which food and drink are consumed, in short all the underlying cultural assumptions need to be brought out if one wishes to make a good impression on representatives of another culture. One can never be completely sure one will do the right thing, so one should also develop strategies for apologizing for unintentional affronts.

21 We are looking for synonyms of words for *rain, sleet, snow, hail,* etc. *Roget's Thesaurus* offers for *rain*: *precipitation; drizzle, mizzle; shower, downpour, drencher, soaker, cloudburst; flurry,* and then moves into other types of weather.

22 This is another activity that is probably best done in a group. It will probably be found that people do use many non-native words to do with food and drink. In the Netherlands many immigrants have found that the Dutch are often quite curious about foreign foodstuffs, and have started fast-food eating places and restaurants. As to the likelihood of survival, 'acceptance' of a new form as part of the indigenous culture gives the best chance.

23 In *An Eye for an Eye: Crosslinguistic Constraints on the Development of the L2 Lexicon* (Kellerman and Sharwood Smith eds. 1986), Kellerman discusses this problem in depth. The problem is that words and phrases from the mother tongue may sometimes be transferred into English, and sometimes not. How does one know? There is a statistical relationship with the level of familiarity of English of the foreign learner, but not really a one-to-one relationship. Beginners and intermediate learners tend to accept everything as long as it sounds and looks English. Upper intermediate and higher become suspicious and reject everything that resembles 'native language expressions'. The more familiar the advanced learner becomes with English, the more recognition of real English as opposed to translated native language expressions there is.

24 If you have managed to avoid giving away too much information about the backgrounds of your speakers, you will probably find that the left-hand column scores best for those who speak a form of RP/Standard British English (alternatively: Standard American English), assigning the negative scores to dialect speakers and particularly non-native users of English, depending on your testees' familiarity with native varieties of English. The results are probably related to lack of experience with such varieties of spoken English, so that it becomes extra difficult to make sense of what is being said.

Suggestions for further study

The Council of Europe has produced many studies of the problem of intercultural education. These are widely available. A good start may be Micheline Rey *Training Teachers in Intercultural Education?*, Strasbourg 1986.

One of the problems facing Europe is to do with migrant workers. A useful introduction is Louis Porcher *Reflections on Language Needs in the School*, Strasbourg 1980. David Wilkins tackles the same question in a more technical sense in *The Educational Value of Foreign Language Learning*, Strasbourg 1987.

There are useful collections of studies available which may guide the student wishing to study the problems of intercultural communication in more depth. Useful and illuminating are Gail Nemetz Robinson (ed.) *Crosscultural Understanding*, Pergamon Press Ltd 1985, as well as Joyce Merrill Vàldes (ed.) *Culture Bound*, Cambridge University Press 1986. I have found of special interest Michael Byram and Veronica Esarte-Sarries *Investigating Cultural Studies in Foreign Language Teaching*, Multilingual Matters 1991; Michael Byram, Carol Morgan and Colleagues *Teaching and Learning Language and Culture*, Multilingual Matters 1994; and Claire Kramsch *Context and Culture in Language Teaching*, Oxford University Press 1993. Robin Scarcella *Teaching Language Minority Students in the Multicultural Classroom*, Prentice Hall 1990, focuses on the situation in the United States.

Barry Tomalin and Susan Stemplesky *Cultural Awareness*, Oxford University Press 1993, is a very useful collection of ideas and activities for spotting and dealing with cultural differences.

Chapter 2 Aspects of cultural difference

Indeed, my culture is the logic by which I give order to the world. And I have been learning this logic little by little, since the moment I was born, from the gestures, the words, and the care of those who surrounded me; from their gaze, from the tone of their voices; from the noises, the colors, the smells, the body contact; from the way I was raised, rewarded, punished, held, touched, washed, fed; from the stories I was told, from the books I read, from the songs I sang; in the street, at school, at play; from the relationships I witnessed between others, from the judgments I heard, from the aesthetics embodied everywhere, in all things right down to my sleep and the dreams I learned to dream and recount. I learned to breathe this logic and to forget that I had learned it. I find it natural. Whether I produce meaning or apprehend it, it underlies all my interactions. This does not mean that I must agree with all those who share my culture: I do not necessarily agree with all those who speak the same language as I do. But as different as their discourse may be from mine, it is for me familiar territory, it is recognizable. The same is true, in a certain sense, of my culture.
(Raymonde Carroll *Cultural Misunderstandings*, The French American Experience, The University of Chicago Press 1988, p3)

Introduction

In this chapter I will mainly concentrate on those characteristics, based on knowledge and skills, that are largely shared by people belonging to the same nation. In the terms of Philip Riley (1989b – see below), I shall mainly deal with the areas of *know that* and to some extent with *know how*, those areas of human relations which members of a particular culture *know* to be true and those that everybody *knows* are done in a certain way. The relationship between the two is not always very clear, so that attempts at dealing with them as separate issues will sometimes create difficulties. Important in this context is the phenomenon of cultural change and group culture.

Secondly I will discuss a system of analysing these characteristics, which will help to come to grips with cultural differences in the multicultural classroom. In Chapter 4 the influence of 'culture', both group culture and national culture, will be dealt with in the context of negotiating the syllabus for learning English as a lingua franca.

A definition of culture

Anthropologists use 'culture' to refer to the patterns of feeling, thinking and acting that people in the same social environment share and which set them apart from people from another social environment. Culture in this meaning can be defined as the 'software of the mind' (Hofstede 1991), the set of mental rules that govern our everyday behaviour. This is a much wider meaning than is common in most Western countries. Many people tend to reserve the word 'culture' for the products of artists representing the history and development of 'refined taste' over the centuries. This sense of culture is exclusive, only shared by 'our sort of people'. The anthropologists' use of the term is inclusive, and I shall use it in their sense, unless otherwise indicated.

Culture covers three areas of human behaviour. Philip Riley identifies these as follows: culture, he says,

> **includes**
> ***know that***
> **– what individuals believe to be true: their political and religious philosophies, their 'theories' of disease, education, physics, child bearing, hunting, history, geography, etc. (relative permanent background knowledge);**
> ***know of***
> **– current events and preoccupations: what is going on in the society in question (relatively ephemeral background knowledge);**
> ***know how***
> **– skills and competencies: how to act, how to behave appropriately (how to use the telephone, dance, choose a spouse) and how to speak (how to 'thank, greet, tell a story, address a superior ...'), ie communicative competence.**
> **Culture as knowledge, then, is the sum total of the information, beliefs, values and skills one needs to share and apply in the society and the situations in which one finds oneself: it is what I need to know in order to 'make sense' in and out of those situations in the same way as my fellows. (Riley 1989b p488)**

Culture is learned, not inherited. 'The process of growing up includes learning to behave in ways expected by our society. We usually accept group values without much reflection and without awareness that peoples of other cultures may not share these values. If our culture values cleanliness, promptness, and hard work, we try to be clean, prompt, and industrious. We tend to admire people who exhibit these qualities, unless we are in some way alienated from the culture and thus protest against its values.' (Hilgard *et al.* p399)

Culture and society

Man is a peculiar animal: part of his mental make-up insists on reasonable explanations for natural phenomena and another part of him will insist on the presence of outside powers guiding his behaviour at crucial moments. This strange conflict between rational and irrational impulse, between instinctive and reasoned action, is generally thought to be the result of our genetic history.

Historically man has always been on the lookout for 'logical' explanations for various phenomena. Sometimes he went to look for himself, at other times the voice of authority gave him an answer. The voice might speak to him individually, but sometimes it told him to inform the world. This phenomenon is well attested in human history, and has played a powerful role in shaping culture in various parts of the world. The institution attempting to harness and channel the search for explanations and supervise them, so that they would lead into desired directions, is/was religion.

Religious observance serves to create a bond among the people belonging to a particular social group, the inhabitants of a town or a country. This bond also serves to set its adherents apart from the rest of humanity. The next step logically leads to the conviction that, since one is part of this special group, the rest of mankind is of a lower order, which has led to quite horrifying incidents in the history of mankind. In the context of culture the problem with religions is that their representatives generally refuse to consider the alternative point of view as a valuable contribution to the discussion of co-existence (cf. Shapiro 1986). Indeed, a higher authority has told them that their version of how life should be lived is correct. In many countries in Europe the influence of the church is at present mainly indirect. In many Islamic countries this cannot be said.

In the history of western Europe the 'church' incorporated the 'state'. This needed a few centuries to come about, but once the Roman Emperor Constantine realized that he could use the Christians as his allies, the church was on its way. The church became the official religious institution in every country through the support it had gained in the ruling class. It was an institution to be reckoned with, and it was not at all a simple matter to curtail its influence. The history of Henry VIII of England and later the Protestant revolts in northern Europe illustrate the point. And its influence is still very noticeable in many countries.

A definition of man

There are, then, three factors that play a part in the description of a human being. These are not mutually exclusive, but are linked together so that they make it possible to describe the individual. First of all he/she is a 'man', male or female, and has inherited the characteristics that set him/her apart from the other members of the animal kingdom. Human nature means those characteristics and instincts that all humans share and which set them apart from the animals. Many of these are not exclusive to human beings. One characteristic that is unique to us is language. This was claimed by Darwin, but under the influence of behaviourist psychology attempts were made to prove that language is not instinctual but learned behaviour, not very successfully according to Chomsky in his famous review of Skinner's *Verbal Behavior* in 1959. The amount of evidence has since increased tremendously in favour of the existence of a genetically encoded, universal mental grammar which enables all children to learn any language(s) (Jackendoff 1993; Pinker 1994).

Secondly, man is a social animal, ie he/she belongs to a group of people and behaves according to the code agreed by the members of this group. Man's behaviour in this context has much in common with the way animals living in herds behave towards insiders and outsiders. Insiders belong; they know the code towards the leader of the herd. If they are male, they realize that females are not for them to approach, unless the leader is absent or has given permission. With certain types of monkeys, for example, it is quite common for a new leader to exterminate the young, male offspring of his predecessor. In some human societies comparable behaviour can be observed. Outsiders don't belong. Sometimes, to continue the comparison with the animal kingdom, outsiders are tolerated by the herd, but they never quite achieve a place and a role in the life of the herd. They have to observe the code of the herd very strictly: any non-observance is immediately punished by expulsion for a shorter or longer period of time, if not for ever. The code of behaviour – the culture in human terms – is different from human nature on the one hand and from an individual's personality on the other.

Personality, the last factor, refers to the characteristics that set an individual apart from the other members of the social group to which he/she belongs.

> **Even though cultural pressures impose some personality similarities, individual personality is not completely predictable from a knowledge of the culture in which a person is raised, for three reasons: (1) the cultural impacts upon the person are not actually uniform, because they come to him by way of particular people – parents and others – who are not all alike in their values and practices; (2) the individual has some kinds of experiences that are distinctively his own; and (3) the individual, because of the kind of person he is, redefines the roles he is required to fit into. (Hilgard *et al.* p400)**

Symbols, heroes and rituals

Cultural differences show up on different levels. Sociologists generally discuss cultural differences in terms of 'symbols, heroes and rituals'. To outsiders these are immediately obvious as different from their own. This becomes clear as soon as one gives examples, like the national flag symbolizing a country's unity, the chairman's gavel (a 'ceremonial' hammer) in certain contexts indicating a position of authority, or the headscarf many immigrant Islamic women wear to show their background.

Symbols

Symbols are defined as 'words, gestures, pictures or objects that carry a particular meaning which is only recognized by those who share the culture' (Hofstede 1991 p7). Symbols are important to people in the sense that they make recognition of someone belonging to the same 'group' easier. Symbols serve as a point of recognition for insiders, putting outsiders at a disadvantage to some extent. Managers, for example, are these days recognized by their clothing. In the 1930s and later men who had achieved a certain social status used to show this by wearing a hat; those belonging to the lower classes wore caps, of course. On special occasions in many countries, academics who have received a 'chair' wear a gown and cap which other academics are not allowed to wear yet. For years it was fun to observe a certain type of British office worker in bowler hat, pinstriped trousers, and black jacket flourishing his umbrella on his way to the London underground.

Symbols are very important for people serving ceremonial functions in church ceremonies, in political meetings and in many other 'official' gatherings.

Activity 2.1 Draw up a list of symbols used for ceremonial functions in your country, eg in the context of weddings, funerals, political meetings, sessions of law courts, etc. Draw up a similar list for British culture. The comparison will probably mainly show up differences, but are there similarities?[1]

Heroes

Heroes are the persons, dead or alive, real or imaginary, who serve as models for behaviour. To a certain extent they also serve a symbolic function, particularly when their mannerisms are widely imitated, but their influence is different and less noticeable than that of 'symbols'. There are two classes of heroes: those honoured by a society as a whole and those cherished by a particular generation or a particular group within a society.

We may share our heroes with other societies, just as we sometimes share 'symbols'. During World War II Winston Churchill was the hero of the Allies, as was John F Kennedy of the 'free world' in the 1960s, when communism still seemed to threaten democracy. Cult heroes are generally short-lived. Among speed skaters the name of the Norwegian Johann Olav Koss, around 1990, had heroic connotations at least equal to Alberto Tomba's among ski enthusiasts. Koss ended his career with the winter Olympics of 1994 in Lillehammer, Norway. His name will be remembered among speed-skating enthusiasts for some time, but the general public may already have forgotten his name within a year. At one time Fidel Castro assumed heroic proportions in the eyes of many people supporting left-wing political ideas, for his resistance against American influence in the Caribbean. Although he still runs Cuba, Castro's popularity has virtually disappeared.

Activity 2.2 Who are the heroes of your generation? Make a list of them, and compare this list with a representative of a younger or older generation. Do any heroes occur on both lists? Is it possible to explain this phenomenon?[1]

Rituals

Rituals are to do with areas of behaviour, like ways of greeting and saying farewell, and showing respect towards others, ie 'customary' cultural behaviour, both at the level of the individual and at the social level. Individual rituals may acquire symbolic meaning, as with the professional footballer who realizes a link between putting on his left or right shoe first and the outcome of the coming match. Informally, ritual behaviour can be observed in the way we handle knives and forks during a meal, or the way we get dressed in the morning, etc.

Rituals at the social cultural level are immediately noticeable in ceremonial behaviour, for example in religious services and on formal occasions, such as opening or closing a meeting or introducing an official speaker. In the context of sports the ceremony of handing out the winners' medals is a ritual we all recognize, as we do the way Members of Parliament in Britain like to discuss fairly straightforward matters in a language outsiders often hardly understand. An interesting phenomenon in the context of culture is the ritual of 'kissing a friend' upon meeting in public or private. In some countries the occasion demands an exchange of three kisses (France, the Netherlands) whereas in other countries two is the limit (Britain, Germany). The ritual is restricted to behaviour between women, and men towards women: for men to exchange kisses is highly unusual in western Europe. In many eastern European countries, on the contrary, it is quite common on ritual occasions for men to exchange kisses with men.

Activity 2.3 Draw up a list of rituals that apply to you, for example when getting up in the morning, or having a meal, or in your daily work. How much of your ritual behaviour is generally observed in your culture and is in your experience different from rituals observed elsewhere?[1]

Rituals are important in our dealings with fellow countrymen. Forms of spoken or written address, for example, in particular settings make immediately clear to others the speaker/writer's status and consequently how he/she expects to be addressed. This is particularly true of cultures that distinguish polite and familiar pronouns of address. Languages that do not have these may show the required distinction through other means, verbal as well as non-verbal, such as intonation, careful pronunciation, choice of words, morphology and syntax, body posture, or combinations of these.

Many cultures still observe ancient rituals to mark different stages in growing up from being a baby to adulthood. One that is well known is the ritual of circumcision of little boys as a sign that they belong to the Jewish or Islamic community in which they have been born. Sometimes rituals are less immediately obvious, such as when the new pupil is introduced to his new classmates and the rest of the school. Such rituals, in a more recognizable form, are still found at some public schools and university students' clubs.

Activity 2.4 Read the following passage. It describes a boy undergoing a task clearly set by his father to let him prove himself a man and worthy to join the group of people working the machine called Fat Boy. Then, draw up a list of rituals and ceremonies you had to undergo as part of growing up in your culture. Draw up a similar list, based perhaps on your reading, of rituals you know about, observed in British culture.[1]

Father banged the door after me and cut off most of the daylight. All I could see, through the floor joists that had yet to be planked, was the sun shining dustily down between the cracks in the hatchway door.

It was like being in a monster body, under the cold lips of its stomach tank. Iron pipes rose sideways around the walls. Greasy with sealer and smelling of fresh welds, they had the egg stink of fart-gas, and meat turned to mud, and the slippery look of human waterworks. Where the cracks of sun lighted some rusty pipes I could see how these reddened blisters looked like flesh. The smallest movement of my feet made a booming belly-echo. Organs was a good word.

A week before, I had scaled the outside with ease. But this was my first time inside, alone, with the door shut, in the dark, making for the top. I gulped my panic and looked up – the way up was the way out. I started climbing the pipes, through the mid-section, from the tanks Father called the kidneys, across the rusty gizzard to the steel tube he called the gullet. The only sounds that penetrated the walls were Clover's and April's yells as they played with the Maywit kids – in the sunshine.

(...)

It made me dizzy. I could not understand enough of it to feel safe. I thought – You could die here, or – trapped inside – go crazy.

I fought for the door and pushed it open. Below the hatchway were straw hats. Someone – not Father – screeched up at me. They set a ladder against Fat Boy and let me down, and they all looked at my face pretty worriedly.

'He ain't bawling anyway,' Francis Lungley said.

'You're next, Fido,' Father said, and hurried Lungley to the door. 'In you go! Take your time – get acquainted!'

One by one he sent them in, slammed the door and made them climb through the pipes to the top hatchway, so they would not be afraid, except

> **Mrs Maywit, Mrs Kennywick and the children. They said they were willing, but Father said, 'That's all that really counts – willingness.' (Paul Theroux, *The Mosquito Coast*, Penguin Books 1983, pp167–8)**

Symbols, heroes, rituals and culture

Symbols, heroes and rituals function to bind together people who belong to the same nation, but within a nation cultural differences also exist. Different social groups within the same nation will have their own symbols, heroes and rituals. Supporters of football clubs like to show their adherence as loudly and emphatically as they possibly can, which generally gives rise to criticism in the media, followed by police attention, sometimes street fighting and consequent arrests. This signals the cultural togetherness of a particular group within a larger unit. Hooliganism, in this way, is an expression of cultural identity (cf. Buford 1992).

This phenomenon is particularly true of the type of comment *youth culture* gives rise to.

> **Young people are born into and socialised within a particular class culture, but because social conditions change over time, they are also subject to different experiences and influences from their parents. They therefore negotiate space for their own culture (or, more appropriately, *sub*culture) within the parent class culture. The spaces they win include territory like street corners within the locality, time and space for leisure and recreation, and occasions for social interaction (the weekend, the disco, football matches, or standing about doing nothing). (Widdicombe and Wooffitt 1995 p17)**

Activity 2.5 In what ways do young people in your country show they are different from other people, both young and old. What 'symbols' are used to ease cultural identification. Think of items of dress, hairstyle, preferred beverages, choice of words, status symbols, etc. How many of these are shared by other groups?[1]

At moments of confrontation people tend to identify emphatically with their home culture. International sports events are occasions when many people show their cultural allegiance. These are events when feelings of nationalism can be shown at their least harmful. Disasters and wars generally give rise to demonstrations of nationalistic feelings, as if all the people belonging to a nation share the same notions and ideas. This is only partly true, of course. One needs only to think of political meetings at election times to realize that within nations there are large areas of disagreement on many essential issues. All the same, people belonging to the same nation more or less agree on issues of behaviour, both towards fellow countrymen and towards foreigners.

Symbols, heroes and rituals can be observed by an outsider, and have been by sociologists and anthropologists. The most famous study in this area is probably Margaret Mead's *Coming of Age in Samoa*, although heroes play a relatively small part in her study. Obviously the outward phenomena of our ways of dealing with each other are based upon a system of values which may not be immediately apparent, but all the same constantly guide our behaviour, particularly towards outsiders. Sometimes, in meetings between different cultures, it may be necessary to make these explicit in order to prevent problems.

Recently a Dutch football club was negotiating the transfer of an eastern European player through an intermediary. The Dutch representative had reached an oral agreement with the footballer's representative and came back to the Netherlands quite happy about what had been achieved. This happy state did not last very long when he heard through the grapevine that the football player was about to sign a contract with a Spanish club (*NRC-Handelsblad*, 13 August 1992).

Activity 2.6 What would be the status of an 'oral agreement' in your culture? How is this perhaps different in this eastern European country? What could one have done in these circumstances? How should the Dutch representative have dealt with this problem in your opinion (in your culture)?[2]

Culture: accident of history

The people in one country will differ from the people in other countries in terms of the values they adhere to, finding their expression in the symbols they recognize, the heroes they admire and the rituals they observe. Factors giving rise to these are found in a country's history and educational system in the widest sense. The history of the Alsace region illustrates the point. Over time the people living there have had to switch their allegiance several times from France to Germany and the other way round. The local language clearly shows the effects: words borrowed from both languages, many people who speak both French and German, although with a noticeable accent. A large percentage of the population no more than tolerates the government in Paris, but feels more in common with other people living on the Rhine.

Education plays an important part in preparing young people for the roles they are expected to take upon them in adult life. Countries have organized their educational systems in many different ways, often reflecting the influence the upper level of society, the rich and powerful, have managed to hold on to in the running of the country. Familiar examples are to be found in the educational systems of France and England, countries where it is notoriously difficult for 'outsiders' to gain admittance to 'the best schools' and 'the best universities'.

Cultural values are not immutable: changes do come about in time, but it may take a long time for them to be accepted. Students of evolution in the main agree that:

> **... species as a whole do not change gradually. Indeed, large populations are surprisingly resistant to change (ie biological change, *author's note*), contrary to what one might expect from the Darwinian idea of gradual selection. (But cultural change owes much to the way the human brain is organized, *author's note*.) Writing wasn't gradually invented everywhere, but rather by what was probably a small group of tax accountants in Sumer, and then the idea spread around. Mathematics and geometry owe much to what happened on the Greek island of Samos in the sixth century BC among the followers of Pythagoras. Because ideas reproduce themselves in virgin minds, thanks to our passion for new schemata, our thoughts have come to have lives of their own, and thus an evolutionary history of their own.**
> **(Calvin 1986 pp193–4)**

Towards the end of his book William H. Calvin comes to this hopeful conclusion for students of cultural change:

> **Thought, and the cultural improvements that go with it, seem to flourish best in situations involving agriculture, cities, educational systems. Those aren't as likely to be found out on the life-is-hard fringes of the population – they flourish in the parts of the world where making a living is somewhat easier, where the population density is higher, where the rumor mill can pass around ideas more easily. Big central populations may be good setups for rapid cultural evolution, but for biological evolution they spell slowdown – no isolation, no small numbers, no repeated do-or-die waves of selection as on the frontiers.**
> **(Calvin 1986 p364)**

These conditions are present in most of Europe, North America, Australia and New Zealand, and some Asian and African countries. So, how can one go about the study of cultural value systems in order to ease the process of confrontation and gradual acceptance of other cultures?

The study of cultural difference

The value system underlying the way in which organizations work internally has been extensively studied by Hofstede (eg *Cultures and Organisations* 1991). He comes to the conclusion that there are four dimensions of culture relevant for western Europe which can be measured for difference. Following Hofstede's research I propose to discuss the concepts of 'power distance', 'individualism vs collectivism', 'assertiveness vs modesty' and 'avoidance of uncertainty' as measures of cultural difference, and the relevance of these in the classroom behaviour of learners and teachers.

The situation in Asia differs in many respects from the Western type of society, not only along these four dimensions. Hofstede in his research discusses a fifth dimension which applies particularly to many Asian countries: 'short-term/long-term focus'. Europeans are typically focused on the short term: 'Life is short, we'll have to get the most out of it while we can.' Asians generally take the long-term view: 'After this life there is more to come.' It might be interesting to speculate on what would change in our, western European, dealings with the environment, if we accepted a more 'long-term focus' than we do now. An important proviso should be made, however. Although these five dimensions are helpful in characterizing a culture, as soon as one applies them to individual members of this culture there may be clear divergences. Asians, for example, are said to take the long-term view, but some Asian societies are rapidly changing, with individual members adopting a 'get rich quick mentality' and losing the long-term focus, reminding us that culture is not a static phenomenon, but is always changing.

Power distance

Societies as they exist today have been shaped by their histories. Internal relationships within each society may seem stable, but clearly depend for their continuation or change on the relations among the individuals making up that society. It is in the interest of some people to keep relations as they are, whereas it is in the interest of others to rock the boat, if they can. Some societies are more tolerant of change than others.

Humans are not born equal. Everyone is aware of individual differences, caused by personality characteristics or physical abilities, such as intelligence and strength, or by income and/or family background, etc, but is it necessary that a person through the accident of having been born into a particular family should enjoy privileges denied other members belonging to that particular society? Authority, the power to take decisions affecting others, is a feature of all societies. But some societies regulate the lives of those belonging to their sphere of influence more than others on the basis of authority. In other societies the principle of a negotiated agreement between the parties involved is strictly adhered to, and in still other societies it is totally flouted.

Power distance is a measure of built-in inequality. The effects of power distance show themselves in the way people in influential positions are treated by their environment. In the Scandinavian countries democracy has worked for many years. The inhabitants tend to be less impressed by the function of the Prime Minister than by his/her personality. They are/must be on the whole easily approachable people who do not give the impression that the country would go to the dogs without them; an impression one often takes away from Prime Ministers' behaviour in, particularly, southern and eastern European, and many other, countries.

Activity 2.7 What arguments are usually brought forward to defend the moral right of people in positions of power to enjoy the privileges they have in your country? To what extent is there general agreement with this situation?[3]

Reserving certain privileges for certain functions in society is a custom as old as humanity, probably. The phenomenon can be found in all walks of life. The chairperson in a meeting is often equipped with a gavel as a symbol of authority. The chairperson's power is restricted to the meeting, except perhaps where he/she claims the function on the grounds of authority in other settings not directly related to the function of the meeting. Kings and queens have thrones and crowns and other regalia to symbolize their roles. The ceremonies and rituals surrounding their public duties are closely observed in many countries, but not in all.

Symbols such as those referred to here and their attending privileges are characteristic of certain societies. Immutable rights of certain groups of people, such as those derived from attendance at an 'exclusive' educational institution, will lead to recognizable patterns of behaviour in the community of which they are a part. They are apparent in the way people deal with each other – and reflected in measures of power distance. They are also part of language behaviour. (See the section on *Social relationships* in this chapter.) *The Oxbridge Conspiracy* (Ellis 1994) describes and analyses in detail the old-boy network that runs Great Britain and has run it for many, many years. The kind of networking Ellis describes is, of course, to a greater or lesser extent present in all walks of life. It ensures that members of the network have access to certain advantages, while outsiders do not.

Activity 2.8 If you are a member of a network such as a sports club, or another organization that goes in for competitions, draw up a list of privileges of members of the first team. Why would such privileges be considered necessary?

Individualism and collectivism

Human beings are individuals, ie they are uniquely different from other individuals, and at the same time they share many characteristics with other members of their social group. Often they will allow themselves to be led by one member of the group, while at other moments they will insist on taking their own decisions. In this context the novelist Frank Herbert commented:

> ***Dune*** **was aimed at this whole idea of the infallible leader because my view of history says mistakes made by a leader (or made in a leader's name) are amplified by the numbers who follow without question.**
>
> **That's how 900 people wound up in Guyana drinking poison Kool-Aid.**
>
> **That's how the US said 'Yes, sir, Mister Charismatic John Kennedy!' and found itself embroiled in Vietnam.**
>
> **That's how Germany said '*Sieg Heil!*' and murdered more than six million of our fellow human beings.**
>
> **Leadership and our dependence on it (how and why we choose particular leaders) is a much misunderstood historical phenomenon.**
>
> **(Herbert and Herbert 1987 p13)**

The amount of individual freedom and the space where individuals follow the directives of others can and will be manipulated, depending on circumstances and individuals. In every community a balance has to be found between the needs of each individual and the needs of the collective, the community as a whole. Some cultures emphasize individuality more, while others favour the collective.

Activity 2.9 Read the following text and decide on the writer's attitude towards the proceedings, if possible comparing your conclusions with others'.

> **I had always assumed that a sporting event was a paid-for entertainment, like a night at the cinema; that it was an exchange; you gave up a small part of your earnings and were rewarded by a span (an hour, two hours) of pleasure, frequently characterized by features – edible food, working lavatories, a managed crowd, a place to park your car – that tended to encourage you to return the following week. I thought this was normal. I could see that I was wrong. What principle governed the British sporting event? It appeared that, in exchange for a few pounds, you received one hour and forty-five minutes characterized by the greatest possible exposure to the worst possible weather, the greatest number of people in the smallest possible space and the greatest number of obstacles – unreliable transport, no parking, an intensely dangerous crush at the only exit, a repellent polio pond to pee into, last minute changes of the starting time – to keep you from ever attending a match again.**
>
> **And yet, here they all were, having their Saturday.**
>
> **(Buford 1992 p19)**

What moved the author to undergo this experience? What would have moved the crowd to accept the conditions as they are at the football stadium? Would you accept them?[4]

The United States of America is probably a good example of an individualistic society and China of a collectivist one. The point is that every national culture, programmed by incidents in the collective experience, is traditionally more or less predisposed towards individualism or collectivism. The same is true of each individual human being. There are moments when we instinctively follow the direction of the herd, and others where we prefer our personal inclinations. To some extent traditional attitudes can be changed through pressure exerted by the existing power structure, but whether this will lead to lasting change is uncertain. Former communist countries were firmly collectivist in outlook, but today individualism seems to have gained favour again.

The difference between the two types of society was illustrated in the experience of the Dutch football club above (page 34). Philip Riley draws attention to the fact that within a society collectivism may also be very much present, particularly among people belonging to a specific calling. This shows itself most clearly in the context of Language for Specific Purposes. 'Doctors do not always share their knowledge with their patients, nor do policemen interrogating witnesses, or examiners questioning students, or second-hand car salesmen. (...) One of the most common motives for withholding knowledge is that its possession confers an advantage of some kind, very often social or financial.' (Riley 1989c p72)

Assertiveness vs modesty

Some aspects of individualism and collectivism are to do with the traditional roles of men and women in society.

Activity 2.10 Read the following text. Would the behaviour described in the passage be acceptable in your culture? What societies/cultures, to your knowledge, would find this type of behaviour 'normal'?

> **For my great-grandfather, this was a once-in-a-lifetime chance, the closest he was ever going to get to a real VIP. He schemed to get himself the job of escorting General Xue, and told his wife he was going to try to marry their daughter to him. He did not ask his wife for her agreement; he merely informed her. Quite apart from this being the custom of the day, my great-grandfather despised his wife. She wept, but said nothing. He told her she must not breathe a word to their daughter. Marriage was a transaction, not a matter of feelings. She would be informed when the wedding was arranged.**
> **(Jung Chang, *Wild Swans*, Flamingo, HarperCollins Publishers 1991, p36.)[5]**

Men, traditionally in most cultures, are expected to assert themselves, to insist on having their way in family matters, to enjoy certain rights at home – like receiving the best possible education the parents can afford – simply because they are males. Women, on the other hand, are expected to be submissive, to comply with having a lower status, to look after the other members of the family before promoting their own interests, in short to be modest. Hofstede makes the point that of course there are, and always have been, assertive females and submissive men. The point at issue is what is expected of men and women in a particular society.

Avoidance of uncertainty

The final concept, 'avoidance of uncertainty', is also related to power. It is a measure of the tolerance of ambiguity within a society. Some people become very anxious when confronted with a problem they can't decide on the basis of existing rules, while others are completely happy to use their own initiative in order to solve the same problem. Some communities accept that one can't foresee every eventuality and prefer to provide broad guidelines, while other communities are the exact opposite. They will supply detailed prescriptions for every eventuality; sometimes with the result that there are so many rules that nobody bothers to follow them anyway.

Activity 2.11 Read the following extract and consider whether this type of discussion involving the same personnel could occur, given a similar situation, in your culture. In particular, have a close look at the relationship between the 'commissaris' and the 'public prosecutor' in the text. In the Dutch context the public prosecutor is the public authority responsible for taking judicial action. In that capacity he is placed above the commissaris (a high-ranking police official: Chief of Police) who is responsible for collecting the necessary evidence. In that sense there is no ambiguity as to who should be responsible for whatever action is decided. But, apparently, this is not quite clear in the setting introduced here. How do the public prosecutor and the commissaris deal with 'uncertainty avoidance'?

The red light attached to the commissaris' office door was on and his telephone was, temporarily, disconnected. No one, except the chief constable – who could press a special button that engaged the buzzer near the commissaris' desk – could disturb him now. The commissaris was facing his three visitors. 'Yes,' the commissaris said, addressing the public prosecutor, a man in his late forties, conservatively dressed in a dark blue suit, white shirt and gray tie, 'I know this isn't the usual procedure but I asked these two detectives in because I value their insight and advice.'

The public prosecutor nodded, Grijpstra smiled and de Gier looked noncommittal. 'I appreciate the company of the two gentlemen,' the public prosecutor said slowly, 'and the matter is serious enough. We are, after all, trying to reach a decision about the liberty of a human being, and liberty is the greatest good.'

'Yes,' the commissaris said quietly.

'But there's something about this I don't like so much,' the public prosecutor said and the laugh wrinkles around his eyes suddenly became very noticeable.

'Yes?' the commissaris asked.

'It seems that I am being asked what *I* think about the possible guilt of Miss Mary van Krompen,' the public prosecutor said. 'Your approach should have been different. You should have tried to *prove* the guilt of the lady to me. You should have been questioning her now for two days and you can't hold her any longer on your own authority. All right. So now my office has to approve her remaining in custody. Fine. The police tell us about their suspicions, the various facts are outlined, we read through the reports of the interrogators, and we make up our mind.'

'Yes?' the commissaris asked.

'Yes. But this time you ask *me* what I think. Are you in doubt about what you should do?'

The commissaris nodded gravely. 'Yes, I am in doubt. Very much so.'

'Why? The facts seem clear enough. Footprints, nice clear plaster of Paris footprints matching the lady's shoes. The lady admits that she saw

the corpse but she didn't contact the police; that's a crime in itself and I hope you'll charge her with it. And on top of it all the unbelievable accuracy of the shot. A thirty-three foot distance between weapon and wound according to the experts and the victim didn't just stand there waiting to be shot between the eyes. He must have moved when he realized his life was in danger. The killer can't have had more than a few seconds to pull the trigger. Wernekink wasn't tied to a stake, was he, or blindfolded?' The public prosecutor was working himself up into a rage, acting his part at court, facing the judges and the lawyer defending the accused.

'Ah, hum,' the public prosecutor said, 'excuse me, I was being carried away by the clear implications of the evidence facing us. Still, the evidence *is* undeniable, isn't it? And the lady is a crack shot; she won a number of prizes and she is the champion of her club.'

'Yes, sir,' the commissaris said, 'she is a champion; she is also a lesbian, and the girl making up to the neighbour – a girl living in her house as a lodger – is very attractive. But there is no conclusive evidence, I think. No, not conclusive. The lady swears she didn't do it.'

(Jan Willem van de Wetering, *The Corpse on the Dike*, Pocket Books 1978, pp44–6)[6]

Cultural differences measured along these dimensions

The interplay among these four dimensions produces the differences between various cultures. Had other dimensions (than Hofstede's) been used, other differences would have resulted. The important thing to remember is that there would have been differences all the same. Broad generalizations about cultural differences between nations are possible, but within nations there will be differences among groups along the same lines.

A high score on the dimension of power distance correlates significantly with a high score on the dimension of uncertainty avoidance. Southern European countries are said to favour clear power structures, a fair amount of collectivism and assertiveness particularly among the male section of the population, and to prefer to avoid uncertainty. Northern European countries in many respects seem to be the exact opposite. Status does not automatically carry privileges; men and women have equal rights; and individual initiative is generally appreciated. These countries mainly score low on the dimension of uncertainty avoidance and around average on the collective/individualist dimension. Hofstede (1991) notes that the borderline between northern and southern cultural differences coincides with the frontiers achieved by the Roman Empire, and particularly in western Europe with the dividing line between a southern part which mainly supports the Roman Catholic Church and the Protestant north.

Social relationships

Languages to a large extent reflect the way a society deals with the four dimensions discussed. Power distance is apparent in the distinction many languages show in the use of second person pronouns: one form for persons close to the speaker and another for people who are distant, mainly because of social status, age, or simply because they are outside the speaker's sphere of close relations and friends. An extreme example of the *tu/vous* (T/V) distinction is a family which uses *tu* for members of the immediate family only, reserving *vous* for in-laws as well as other outsiders. More typically, the French include in-laws and friends in the T category and address unknowns and those in positions of power as V.

Forms of 'polite address' are available in all languages, of course, although perhaps not as explicitly in the lexical system as in the case of *tu/vous*.

Activity 2.12 Many languages distinguish between 'familiar' and 'polite' forms of address. If your native language has the distinct forms, does the distinction made above for French apply to your language, or is it in some respects different? Has there been any notable change in use over the past fifty years?[7]

Manipulation

Native speakers will use a variety of means (verbal as well as non-verbal) to manipulate an interlocutor to achieve their objective, naturally. Manipulation works two ways, as we all know. A 'powerful' person will use the means at his disposal to achieve his goals. One of the ways to make a person do something is to promise a reward in one form or other. The opposite also occurs: dire threats, if one does not support a particular plan or proposal. People without power will use flattery and/or bribes to achieve their goals. Corruption is a phenomenon outsiders generally take note of in a society where power distance is fairly large. In countries where power distance is small, the normal way of going about winning someone's support is by negotiation, arguing one's case and thus hoping to find a compromise that all the parties involved will agree to.

A free press may be an instrument in bringing about cultural changes, eg in the existing power structure. Quite often those in power will try to manipulate the media into distributing certain types of information and withholding others. If power distance and collectivism both score high in a particular country, the press will be totally unreliable. If these dimensions score fairly low, there is a chance that the media are 'free'. There are then few problems with reliability of news coverage: some journalist will almost certainly turn up what someone in a position of power was trying to cover up. Instances of attempts at manipulation of the media abound in many countries.

Activity 2.13 Recently a British journalist who refused to reveal his source of a certain news item had to take his case to the European Court of Justice in Luxemburg. Asked to comment, a Swedish journalist said that protection of sources in his country was no problem at all, that, in fact, it was a reasonably common experience for a government official to read out, over the telephone, the text of a not-yet-made-public document to him or to another journalist, and, if this led to publication, it would have no consequences for anyone involved (a BBC documentary, Standing up to the State, broadcast on Saturday 20 May 1995). Clearly, the situation with regard to the issue of 'protection of sources' may differ from one country to another. It is an indication of the score of power distance and collectivism in a country.

What is the situation in your country with regard to 'protection of sources' by the media? Using a ten-point scale, putting great power distance and a high level of individualism at 10 points, where would you place your country on these scales?

Consult note 8 and the information provided on these two measures for many countries. Does your estimate agree with Hofstede's research? Can you account for the difference if any?[8]

Conditions where the survival of the group depends on the contributions of every member of the group will bring about a collectivist frame of mind. This is particularly true in times of war. At such times power may well be concentrated in the hands of very few individuals. Once achieved it is understandably very difficult to relinquish this position and return power to the community. Throughout history people in power have sought to keep such a position for themselves and, if possible, for their descendants.

In areas where the climate is harsh and in consequence the population thinly spread, mutual dependence is often in evidence. At the same time there is more room for individual initiative. Consequently there will be more of a balance between collectivism and individualism. Once the possible threat to a community has gone, as for example in the United States during the 18th century, and the climate is right, individualist tendencies can come to the fore. But even in the USA this could only be achieved through a revolt against the British. History shows numerous examples of societies where the existing order was swept away, more or less brutally.

Activity 2.14 Think of one or two examples of historic changes in your country, where the people in power had to make room for others. Was the change as fundamental as the people looking for change had intended? If you are not sure, check with a history book. Have you any explanations as to the lack of fundamental change?[9]

Education: its role in shaping social relationships

Education used to be one of the prerogatives of the church. The privilege served two functions: on the one hand education made it possible for the church to find the necessary people to carry out the job of running the church and at the same time it provided an *entrée* into the corridors of power, if and when it was felt that certain measures should be taken, or not taken, which were detrimental to the continuation of the function of the church within (a particular) society.

In western Europe nowadays education is the concern of the state. '*Education* serves the State by fulfilling three functions. These are economic-reproductive (a process of qualification for work in the economy), ideological (the inculcation of attitudes and values), and repressive (the imposition of sanctions for not complying with the demands of the school. In many countries there is no alternative to the education offered by the State)' (Phillipson 1992 p68). This does not always mean that the state supervises all types of education closely. It usually implies, at least in most of western Europe, setting basic requirements for teacher qualifications, diplomas, school buildings, minimum numbers of pupils/students, subjects taught, and so on. In many countries the Ministry of Education has very little to say on how the set subjects are taught. Methodology is the teacher's choice, although there may be some form of indirect influence.

This 'benevolent' type of supervision allows parents to choose the school they want for their children and, indeed, to organize a school themselves as long as it meets the state-set requirements. British parents can, and many do, choose to send their children to a public school, ie a fee-paying school, if they have the money, thus setting them on the road to a (hopefully) influential position in society once they are qualified.

Other countries, eg the Netherlands, have organized primary education for all, and 'stream' their secondary education (since 1993 the first three years have followed the same syllabus in virtually all types of secondary education). There is a possibility of private schooling, but children sent there have generally failed in the state system.

Activity 2.15 How is education organized in your country? Does religious denomination play any part in parents' choice of school? Does the system allow for 'sending the children of the "best" social class to the "best" type of school'? What influences parents' choice of school? Why would some parents decide to pay for their children's education when the state provides it for free? Do the schools deliver what they promise?[10]

It has often been said that in order for a country to function as a democracy its inhabitants must have achieved a minimum level of education and income. If all one's energy and time are occupied finding sufficient food for the family, there is no time nor energy left for taking part in the running of the community. Western Europe has left this stage long behind. Almost everyone can afford a holiday each year, and finds it necessary to have one with the family. It has been a long time since people died from malnutrition.

In many countries the traditional power structure, including the traditional alternatives, is under pressure. But change is a slow process, a process that will be influenced by the way history has given shape to the power structure in a country. Different cultures deal in different ways with 'powerful' institutions and the ways in which they maintain existing power relationships. The influence of a country's power structure shapes to a very large extent our system of values, basically through insisting on the use of certain rituals, and quite often deciding for us who are our heroes, and what symbols we must use in what circumstances.

Activity 2.16 Where in your view does your country stand with regard to the four dimensions of 'power distance', 'collectivism', 'assertiveness' and 'uncertainty avoidance'? How would you, impressionistically, judge other countries in Europe on the basis of these dimensions? Check your impressions, if necessary, with the information provided in note 8. What would be the result for the type of education you would find in these countries?[8]

Language and cultural difference

The study of language has traditionally mainly been concerned with the study of structure – grammar, if you like – and hardly with the study of language use, ie analysis of discourse. From a social point of view this last area is by far the most interesting, because it shows up how people actually use language as 'the primary medium of social control and power' (Fairclough 1989 p3). It is through our use of language that we show others who we are and what we are. In fact, in order to arrive at the social position that we occupy we must have mastered the language that is appropriate to that position. This is particularly true of positions that involve power: doctors, lawyers, politicians, teachers, for example, but perhaps less of computer programmers and other specialists in a restricted service area, like car mechanics or building experts.

Activity 2.17 The following dialogue, taken from Fairclough 1989 p18, is part of an interview in a police-station, involving the witness to an armed robbery (W) and a policeman (P), in which basic information elicitation is going on. W, who is rather shaken by the experience, is being asked what happened. P is recording the information in writing.

(1) P: Did you get a look at the one in the car?
(2) W: I saw his face, yeah.
(3) P: What sort of age was he?
(4) W: About 45. He was wearing a ...
(5) P: And how tall?
(6) W: Six foot one.
(7) P: Six foot one. Hair?
(8) W: Dark and curly. Is this going to take long? I've got to collect the kids from school.
(9) P: Not much longer, no. What about his clothes?
(10) W: He was a bit scruffy-looking, blue trousers, black ...
(11) P: Jeans?
(12) W: Yeah.

In what respects is this conversation different from an ordinary one? You may find it helpful to begin the analysis using Hofstede's four dimensions to define the relationship between W and P, using phrases from the dialogue to support your opinion. How would you like to change the wording of P to make the relationship between the speakers more 'equal'? Would a policeman in your country behave in the same way? If not, in what way would he treat a potential witness differently?[11]

Language and social intercourse

The field of discourse analysis gradually provides us with insights into the relationship between language and power, and the linguistic tricks we get up to to continue existing social relations. I will return to this topic in the following chapters. For the moment I would like to point out that in the field of foreign language learning and teaching we have tended to underestimate the problem of becoming part of another culture, simply because we have concentrated on teaching 'form' and perhaps paid too little attention to 'function'.

Country and language have been linked for many years. Every country has its 'standard language', the standard language being the variant with few regional and working-class markers, ie the way the ruling classes form and pronounce words and phrases. This standard form is the language taught in schools, preferably used in broadcasting, the code used by newspapers and more or less official publications. In most countries central governments behave as if there is only the one language spoken within the borders of the country. At the same time there is no country in Europe where only one single language is spoken by all the inhabitants.

Attitudes of governments change occasionally, but only slowly. Many countries in western Europe have by now recognized that in a democracy minority languages will insist upon their democratic rights. This has meant that Welsh is now on the school curriculum in Wales and Gaelic is accepted in Ireland, and that in Germany Plattdeutsch was used in a formal debate in Parliament recently.

Now that the European Union seems to be taking shape, it is interesting to follow the discussions concerning which languages will be used in official publications and settings. None of the smaller countries will accept the dominance of the big languages (German, French and English). They will, and do, insist on their rights *vis à vis* their big brothers. In fact, a special languages programme – LINGUA – was started by the Council of Ministers of the European Community (EC) to promote the learning of foreign languages within the community, with preferential treatment for 'the least used and least taught languages'.[12] At the same time, English occupies such a position of power that at least one government has found it necessary to introduce special legislation to counter the growing use of English and American replacing native terminology.

Conclusion

Hofstede (1993) discusses the problem of finding a balance among the five dimensions he and others have so widely researched. His conclusion is somewhat pessimistic with regard to the amount of time needed to change the mental programming of the citizens of Europe. Perhaps some slow change can be achieved through education, particularly if one of its aims is to help young Europeans find their place in the European community and generally achieve a happy existence.

Power distance in particular plays its part in the relationships between persons, often causing trauma and feelings of aggression. Circumstances may not permit a person or a group of persons to give utterance to feelings of aggression, but the feeling is there, waiting for a chance to come out. All human beings, as every psychiatrist can tell, have a need to be 'recognized', to be respected as individuals. Whenever people are treated in a way that shows no respect for their humanity, the outcome is frustration, often turning into aggression, which can only be prevented by a process of negotiation in which both parties are willing to respect the other and his/her point of view.

Many countries regularly check on the well-being of their citizens. There are a number of indicators that are generally used to find out about the sense of well-being. A reasonable amount of money is often assumed to be necessary, but in actual practice it proves of minor importance. Freedom of choice scores much higher; the freedom of individuals to organize their lives according to their ideas of happiness is an important indicator. Immaterial matters are more important to the well-being of the individual than material things, though it helps to have some money to spend. Educational opportunity and a high level of education are useful indices as well, according to R Veenhoven of the Erasmus University of Rotterdam in a newspaper interview (*De Gelderlander* 9 July 1994).[13]

A comparison of his broad findings with Hofstede's dimensions indicates an interesting educational direction. On each of the dimensions educators should aim for a more or less medial position. Power distance should not be too much of a hindrance in individual development. Someone who is constantly supervised and required to consult his superiors on every decision will not show a great deal of initiative, perhaps not even in his personal life. The same is probably true of the person who must live according to a book full of rules. The society that scores high on collectivism will not allow much individual initiative, and consequently will make many of its people lead unhappy lives. The same is generally true of societies that observe a strict division of roles, and labour, between men and women.

Activity 2.18 On the basis of the charts provided in note 8, which countries would probably have the happiest population? Does this agree with your perception of the people you happen to know who live in that country? People develop blind spots for such things, because of having grown up in and being conditioned by that culture. What about living in your country? What needs to be done to improve your country's scores on Hofstede's dimensions?[8]

Notes

1 These first activities serve to raise awareness of 'symbols, heroes and rituals' and the way they serve as points of recognition by members of a particular group within a society. At this stage no attempt needs to be made to give structure and coherence to these first impressions. If the activities are used with groups of pupils and/or students it may help to include 'language'. Language use, including accent and dialect, also serves as a recognition signal, perhaps even as a first signal to be followed by others.

2 The football club concerned did very little. They sent a letter to UEFA (Union of European Football Associations) reporting the affair and left it at that. However, according to Roman law, which applies in the Netherlands and in most other countries of Europe, such an oral agreement would be as binding as a written contract. And, had the negotiation been with a representative of a football player native of any western European country, UEFA would have been asked to take action.

3 Often a 'higher authority' is invoked to defend rights that are mainly a leftover from times when it was felt to be necessary to impress those members of the nation without influence and/or voting rights with the importance of a particular functionary. In some countries, for example, Members of Parliament enjoy parliamentary immunity, which in other countries is felt to be absolutely unnecessary. Any attempt at discussing the issue, and doing away with the privilege, is generally quickly squashed, since 'we cannot do our work properly, when ...'

4 The text is from *Among the Thugs*, Mandarin Paperback 1992. Bill Buford is a complete outsider, born and bred in the US, who became engrossed in the phenomenon of crowd behaviour around football matches in Britain. He joined groups of supporters, becoming part of the crowds, and attended football matches in Britain and on the continent, describing his and the other supporters' experiences, until in the end he had had enough and stopped.

5 In many societies the roles of men and women are changing, of course, and in many instances have changed. Men are taking up cooking, cleaning and looking after the children, when women are pursuing their careers. In *Wild Swans* the author describes the changes that involved the lives of 'three daughters of China': herself, her mother and grandmother. Sometimes such changes only affect outward appearance: Russia was a country where both sexes had equal rights. In actual practice, this often meant that women had to do the housework on top of their daily job. This may be true of other countries where tradition is strong, ie where power distance scores high.

6 In Van de Wetering's novels the scene is generally set in Amsterdam, thus the commissaris would have to be someone with very wide experience in matters discussed in this scene. He seems to work 'outside the book' in most of his cases, as he does in this one. At the end of the meeting we find the following:

The public prosecutor's mood changed. He remembered the many conversations he had had with the commissaris, both at Headquarters and at home. He also remembered his admiration for the frail old man who so often approached a problem from an unusual, but often correct, angle. He sighed again. 'Well, we'll have to go on with her. We can't let her go. I don't see any possibility of that at all.'

(Wetering 1978 p48).

Clearly, the public prosecutor will allow the commissaris to continue to work *not* according to the rules.

7 According to John Lyons

Social psychologists have investigated the use of T and V in terms of the concepts of power and solidarity, on the one hand, and of reciprocal and non-reciprocal usage, on the other. Generally speaking, we can say that non-reciprocal usage indicates an acknowledged difference of status. In societies in which non-reciprocal usage exists a socially superior, or otherwise more powerful, person will use T to his inferiors, but be addressed by them as V. But non-reciprocal usage has been on the decline in most European languages since the nineteenth century, except in the case of adults and children who are not members of the same family and in one or two more specific cases. This is explained historically in part by the spread of more egalitarian or democratic attitudes in Western societies and in part by the increased importance of the solidarity factor, marked not simply by reciprocal usage as such, but more particularly by the reciprocal use of T.

(Lyons, *Language and Linguistics*, Cambridge University Press 1981, p318)

Note: 'T' refers to more or less equivalent forms of French *tu*, and 'V' to *vous*.

8 Hofstede in his research compared the four dimensions, finding the following results:

Table 1 Abbreviations for the countries and regions studied

Abbreviation	*Country or region*	*Abbreviation*	*Country or region*	*Abbreviation*	*Country or region*
ARA	Arab-speaking countries (Egypt, Iraq, Kuwait, Lebanon, Libya, Saudi Arabia, United Arab Emirates)	GBR	Great Britain	PAN	Panama
		GER	Germany	PER	Peru
		GRE	Greece	PHI	Philippines
		GUA	Guatemala	POR	Portugal
		HOK	Hong Kong	SAF	South Africa
ARG	Argentina	IDO	Indonesia	SAL	Salvador
AUL	Australia	IND	India	SIN	Singapore
AUT	Austria	IRA	Iran	SPA	Spain\
BEL	Belgium	IRE	Ireland (Republic of)	SWE	Sweden
BRA	Brazil	ISR	Israel	SWI	Switzerland
CAN	Canada	ITA	Italy	TAI	Taiwan
CHL	Chile	JAM	Jamaica	THA	Thailand
COL	Columbia	JPN	Japan	TUR	Turkey
COS	Costa Rica	KOR	South Korea	URU	Uruguay
DEN	Denmark	MAL	Malaysia	USA	United States
EAF	East Africa (Ethiopia, Kenya, Tanzania, Zambia)	MEX	Mexico	VEN	Venezuela
		NET	Netherlands	WAF	West Africa (Ghana, Nigeria, Sierra Leone)
EQA	Equador	NOR	Norway		
FIN	Finland	NZL	New Zealand	YUG	Yugoslavia
FRA	France	PAK	Pakistan		

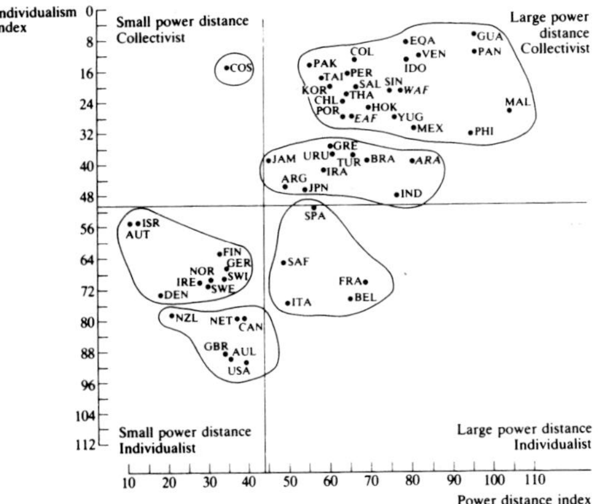

Figure 2 The position of 50 countries and 3 regions on the power distance and individualism–collectivism dimensions (for country name abbreviations see Table 1)

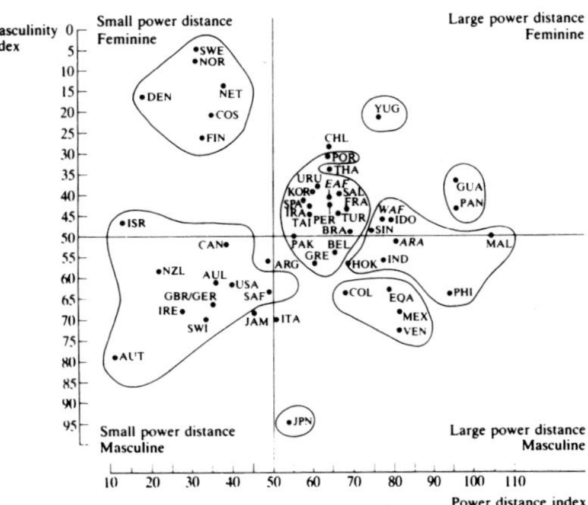

Figure 3 Power distance versus masculinity index scores for 50 countries and 3 regions

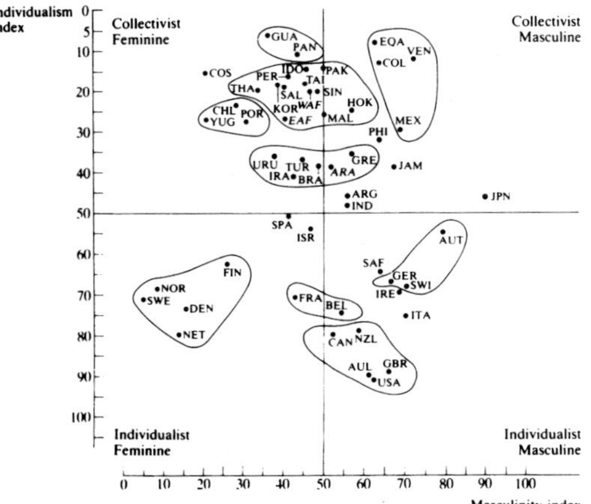

Figure 4 The position of 50 countries and 3 regions on the masculinity–femininity and individualism–collectivism dimensions

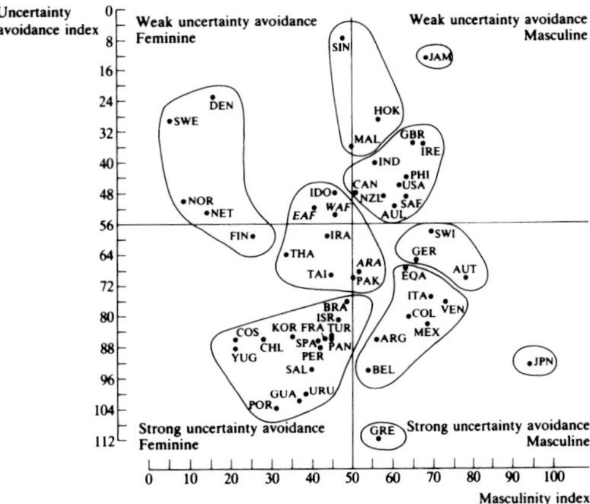

Figure 5 The position of 50 countries and 3 regions on the masculinity/femininity and uncertainty avoidance dimensions

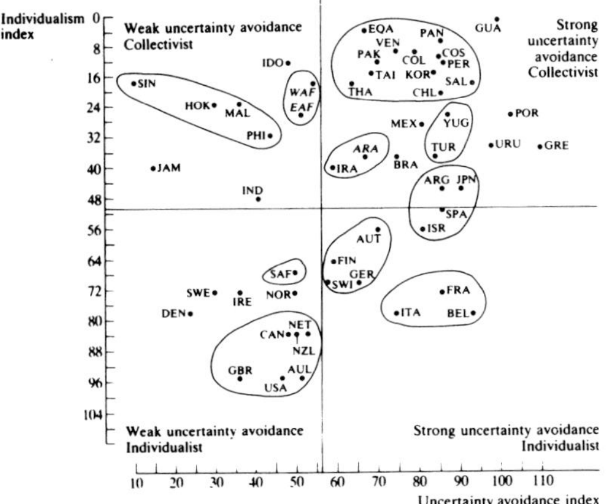

Figure 6 The position of 50 countries and 3 regions on the uncertainty avoidance and individualism–collectivism dimensions

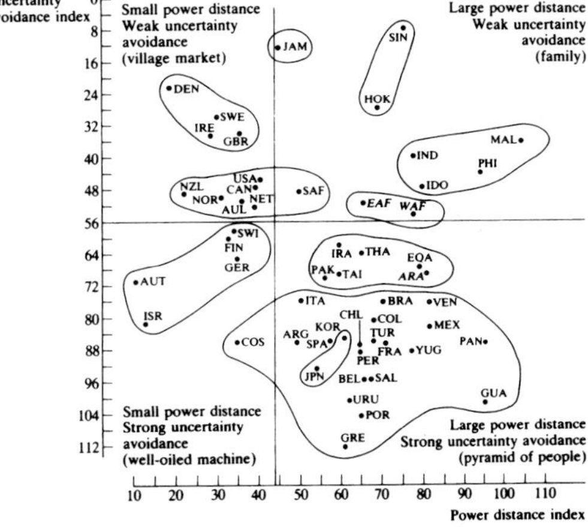

Figure 7 The position of 50 countries and 3 regions on the power distance and uncertainty avoidance dimensions

9 In present-day Russia, after the collapse of communism, it is remarkable that power distance is as large as ever. In order to achieve status in the past one had to be accepted as a party member. Now being a Member of Parliament confers status and power. Very few MPs give the impression that they behave as representatives of the people who voted for them. The problem now seems to be that there is no institution that automatically provides entry into the corridors of power, comparable to the British public schools or the French *Grandes Ecoles*.

10 The Dutch have organized education in their own unique way by providing state education for all, while at the same time accepting schools run by a church (Roman Catholic or Protestant) or by private enterprise (eg 'free' schools are run by a foundation to which parents contribute). When they conform to a number of requirements set by the state, they will receive a subsidy equal to the subsidies state schools receive. Parents are of course part of the power structure in a country. They will therefore send their children to the school that provides the best entry into this structure that they can afford. It is only rarely that they opt for the type of education that will give their child an opportunity to discover and develop their talents.

11 Fairclough comments:

The relationship is an unequal one, with the police interviewer firmly in control of the way the interview develops and of W's contribution to it, and taking no trouble to mitigate the demands he makes of her. (...) In some cases, questions are reduced to words or minimal phrases – *how tall* in turn 5, and *hair* in turn 7. Such reduced questions are typical when one person is filling in a form 'for' another, as P is here; what is interesting is that the sensitive nature of the situation does not override the norms of form-filling. It is also noticeable that there is no acknowledgement of, still less thanks for, the information W supplies. Another feature is the way in which the interviewer checks what W has said in 7. Notice finally how control is exercised over W's contributions: P interrupts W's turn in 5 and 11, and in 9 P gives a minimal answer to W's question about how much longer the interview will take, not acknowledging her problem, and immediately asks another question, thus closing off W's interpellation. (pp18–19)

Changes might be eg (1) Did you by any chance manage to get a good look at the one in the car? (3) What age would you say he was? (5) Excuse me, but could we deal with one thing at a time? You see I have to follow the order of questions on the list. How tall would you say he was? Etc.

Whether the average policeman in your country would deal with a witness differently from the British policeman in this interview would partly depend on factors to do with relative status, ie power distance and the other dimensions, and partly on the way the police in your country perceive their role in society, ie are they there to serve the public and do they act accordingly? Norman Fairclough, *Language and Power*, Longman 1989, provides many instances of language use in British English to gain or impose the upper hand in various social settings through language.

12 LINGUA is only one of the programmes of the European Commission to promote contacts among member states of the EU. Information on these programmes can be obtained at the European Office in the member state one happens to live in, or at Info Point Europe, Schumanplein 12, B-1049 Brussels.

13 Dr Veenhoven has made his research available in the World Database of Happiness (Internet).

Suggestions for further study

Geert Hofstede's study, *Cultures and Organizations, Software of the Mind* (McGraw-Hill International 1991), though it has its methodological limitations, is a must for everyone interested in the way people deal with social relationships and the sharing of power.

Bill Buford, *Among the Thugs* (Mandarin Paperbacks 1992), describes in depth the experience of becoming a football hooligan and the shock of finding out how society deals with crowd violence. Another interesting contribution is Sue Widdicombe and Robin Wooffitt, *The Language of Youth Subcultures* (Harvester Wheatsheaf 1995). They study the problem from the sociologists' point of view.

Cultures have been studied and described from various points of view. A Dutchman, GJ Renier, had a good look at British culture in *The English: Are they Human?* (Ernest Benn 4th ed.1956), of which the first edition appeared in 1931. More recent are Anthony Sampson's studies of British life and society, of which *The Changing Anatomy of Britain*, (Vintage Books Edition 1984) is still useful, as is his *The Midas Touch* (Coronet Books 1989). This last covers a broader perspective than his studies of Britain and is particularly concerned with the relationship between money and power. Ann Barr and Peter York poked glorious fun at the British way of life in *The Official Sloane Rangers Handbook* (Ebury Press 1982). Its subtitle nicely gives away the message: 'The first guide to what really matters in Life.' 'The bizarre rituals and curious customs that make the English English' are extensively covered in Nigel Barley's book, *Native Land* (Penguin Books 1990).

Raymonde Carroll, *Cultural Misunderstandings* (The University of Chicago Press 1988) has an anthropologist's look at the 'French-American Experience'.

Norman Fairclough deals more specifically with the way we use language to maintain or express power in his book *Language and Power* (Longman Language in Social Life Series, 1989). For a discussion of recent developments in the field of discourse analysis Evelyn Hatch, *Discourse and Language Education* (Cambridge University Press 1992), and Michael McCarthy, *Discourse Analysis for Language Teachers* (Cambridge University Press 1993), or Michael McCarthy and Ron Carter, *Language as Discourse: Perspectives for Language Teaching* (Longman 1993) should prove very useful.

Chapter 3 English and the classroom

Since World War II, medicine has undergone great change, in two successive waves. The first was an outpouring of knowledge, techniques, and methods, beginning in the immediate post-war period. It was initiated by the introduction of antibiotics, continued with understanding of electrolyte balances, protein structure, and gene function. For the most part, these advances were scientific and technical, but they changed the face of medical practice drastically, until by 1965 three of the four most prescribed drug classes – antibiotics, hormones (mostly The Pill), and tranquillizers – were all post-war innovations.

The second wave was more recent and involved social, not technical, change. Social medicine, and socialized medicine, became real problems to be solved, like cancer and heart disease. Some of the older physicians regarded socialized medicine as a cancer in its own right, and some of the younger ones agreed. But it has become clear that, like it or not, doctors are going to have to produce better medical care for more people than they ever have before.
(Michael Crichton, *A Case of Need*, Signet Books 1969, pp201–2)

Introduction

Like medicine, the world of language teaching has undergone great changes since World War II. Changes have been of two kinds: first of all the realization has slowly seeped through that learning language(s) is a process set in motion by instinct and not through strict drilling procedures. As in medicine, the second kind of change was social: the realization that in the language-learning process responsibility for making progress must be the learner's, and that the traditional teacher's role must change from instructor to facilitator. Related to both is the shift in emphasis away from written language to learning to communicate orally in the foreign language, which has led to the realization that there are many Englishes, spoken by native speakers and by lingua franca users, and that traditional methodology in no way meets the needs of the communicative classroom.

The debate on 'language as instinct' or 'language as learned behaviour' has virtually run its course. The latest accessible overviews are readily available in Jackendoff (1993) and Pinker (1995). Both agree that the last word has by no means been said yet on the way the language instinct works, but that the evidence for its existence from neurolinguistic research so far is overwhelming.

In this chapter I will discuss the place of English in the European classroom, compared to the other EU languages, and the influence of some varieties of English on the English we may wish to teach in the schools of western Europe. I will also draw attention to methodological developments brought about by the realization that, generally speaking, developing the learner's communicative competence cannot very effectively be done through focusing on grammar and translation (but cf. Rutherford 1987) or pattern drills. In this area the work of the Council of Europe in the field of modern languages is particularly relevant, and due attention will be paid to their work and its influence on the practice of language teaching, as well as to more recent developments (eg Rutherford 1987; McCarthy 1991; Hatch 1992; Nunan 1989, 1991, 1992).

English and the other languages in the European Union

The countries of western Europe share many historical developments and incidents. Economic growth over the past centuries was a matter of co-operative effort, rather than single action, in spite of time-consuming border controls, customs formalities, and different regulations concerning the same product in different countries. Discoveries and inventions quickly spread to neighbouring countries, leading to economic growth for all. Having achieved more or less the same amount of wealth, through mutual trade contacts and exchange of raw materials among other things, it was only natural that after World War II heads of governments should sit together to discuss how developments might be facilitated through doing away with 'protective' economic obstacles between nations.

The millions of people living in Europe belong to different yet related cultural traditions. Societies are based on very similar democratic principles, although at the same time cultural differences abound. In Maastricht (1991) it was agreed to continue the movement towards a unified Europe, which will provide real opportunities to solve problems and conflicts in a peaceful manner. The ongoing process will remain slow. Nations, on the whole, are not led by people who, having achieved a position of authority, voluntarily insist upon sharing the taking of decisions with outsiders, ie members of governments of other countries. Nor do many of them happily hand over control to institutions outside the country. This factor explains why the growth towards European Union is taking far more time and meeting far more obstacles than was hoped at the time the idea was first proposed by Jean Monnet, Robert Schuman, Paul Henri Spaak and all the others who staked their political futures on integrating Europe.

Activity 3.1 You have gained a qualification in teaching EFL in your country. Is it possible, do you think/know, on the basis of that qualification, to work as an EFL teacher in any country of the European Union? Where could you gain information?[1]

Those involved in discussions in a European context quickly find that a solution has to be agreed as to what language to use. People involved in this type of situation are clearly at a disadvantage when they have to communicate in a language not their own. Within the European Union therefore it was a matter of primary interest to agree on a language policy. The Treaty of Rome (1958) agreed on the use of all the languages of the member states as official and as working languages of the European Community and its institutions. This means that all publications are available in each of the nine languages and that all meetings are conducted in all languages, through interpreters. According to the same principle new countries joining the EU will enjoy this right as well, leading to a further increase in work for translators and interpreters. In actual practice of course, the official policy costs money and, whenever it is felt not to be necessary to obey the letter of the treaty, French and English are the languages mainly used. The pressure is on the minority languages to accept their minority status and allow European institutions to do their work in the major languages only.

English, as well as German and French, is one of the majority languages on the basis of a simple head count. Britain's economic influence is probably less than that of Germany, and maybe even of France, in the European context. Within the European context, if not elsewhere, Germany is clearly a force to be reckoned with, and as such can claim a privileged position for its language on school curricula. Economists in the Netherlands are well aware of this, and constantly draw attention to the need of the Dutch worker to be able to communicate in German. Nevertheless, the number of Dutch learners who include German in their study programme has seen a steady decline over the past decade. The same trend is found in other European countries. For French, at least in the Netherlands, a similar trend is noticeable.

Arguments for the inclusion of English in the school curriculum must be derived from its position in the world, rather than its European influence which has been on the wane since the end of the last war. Nevertheless, its position is secure in the curricula of most countries.

English and the world

History is full of surprises. One of the most amazing is how a relatively small island kingdom managed to become a major world power. That is a question historians must answer. It is interesting in the context of this book that the English language shows so much foreign influence in vocabulary and grammar. The population of the British Isles, at any time in its history, adopted words and phrases brought in by foreign visitors and invaders: Celts, Romans, Angles, Saxons, Vikings, French and Normans. Later they also borrowed many words from languages spoken in the former colonies. In this section a thumbnail sketch is presented of historical developments with a view to surveying the present status of the English language in the world.

The American contribution

The growth of English as a world language began with the settlement and colonization of parts of North America. The British government granted charters to British noblemen and chartered companies to set up colonies. These invested money in the colonization of a variety of places along the east coast of North America. The British government kept a watchful eye on developments across the ocean, protected the young colonies against invaders as far as they could, and otherwise left them to their own devices. The various colonies proved to be very attractive to all sorts of groups wishing to leave Europe because of persecution for religious or other reasons, or simply because economic opportunities unavailable in Europe were on offer.

Soon the French and the Dutch joined the colonization movement across the Atlantic. The French settled along the Mississippi River to the south and along the St Lawrence River to the north. The Dutch bought the island of Manhattan from the native population and thus were involved in founding New York. In due course the British brought the whole of North America within their sphere of influence. The language spoken by the colonists shared many characteristics with British English but at the same time used words from Native American languages they came into contact with, and of course many people used words and phrases from their own original languages, particularly when a large group of people in a particular settlement shared the same language background.

After the United States obtained their independence, many colonists, wishing to remain British citizens, moved to Canada, which remained a British colony. With the common border, there was much contact between the two countries, but each took its own course into the future. The Province of Quebec, however, remained mainly French speaking, although the language of education was English until recent years. Experiments in bilingual education are taking place in many parts of Canada, which will hopefully lead to a more peaceful co-existence of the two languages in time.

Over the years the United States has absorbed large numbers of immigrants from all the countries in Europe, pushed into emigration through various economic and other pressures in their native lands. They came from all over in such numbers that even today large sections of some communities firmly link their background to one or other European country. Special mention must be made of the native African part of the population. Originally they were brought in as cheap, unskilled labour, when the southern states flourished as the cotton culture expanded and industry developed. They were mainly supplied through the slave trade. When slavery was abolished in the USA they were free to do the same work as cheap contract labour. It took more than a century for them to acquire the civil rights all the white people naturally had.

The problem of integrating representatives of so many different cultural backgrounds was huge. Much was done through immigrant classes, and insistence on becoming and being a citizen of the USA, but the process of integration was never simple or wholly solved.

The melting pot

Americans often describe their culture as a 'melting pot'. The image suggests that the population has blended well and every segment of American society contributes to the national well-being. As many Americans realize, this is only part of the truth. The original population, the Indians or, as they are mostly called today, Native Americans, refused to give up their way of living and were hounded almost out of existence. Most of the remaining Indians now live on reservations, making themselves 'useful' as a tourist attraction. Only recently have black people in all the states been allowed to exercise their rights as citizens of the United States. The 1960s saw this come about, a century after the black slaves had been freed. These days the southern states have problems coping with the influx of large numbers of Spanish speakers crossing the border from Mexico, looking for work.

The melting pot image holds for much of the white immigrant population. They have shaped American culture into what it is at present, proud of its achievements in the world but at the same time uncertain as to its rights to that position. The United States is slowly facing multiculturalism. Proof of this is that, since 1987, first the State of California, and in the summer of 1991 the State of New York as well, have decided to include a multicultural education programme in the state school curriculum. Other states, among which are Florida, Texas, Minnesota and Washington DC, will follow.

Considering all the influences that have played a part, and still do, in shaping American culture, it is surprising that the language differs only relatively little from its British origin. American English has of course borrowed from native American languages, particularly names of plants, trees and animals not known in Europe, such as: *hickory, persimmon, catalpa, skunk, moose*, and many others. Also various words for types of unfamiliar food, native customs and artefacts were borrowed by the early colonists: *hominy, moccasin, powwow, sachem, toboggan, wigwam*, and so on. Of course, immigrants from various European countries contributed words and sayings, some in the form of literal translations. Dutch words like *cookie, Santa Claus, bowery*, were borrowed; from French came *cache, saloon, poker*; from German *pretzel, kindergarten, spiel*; from Italian *pasta, Mafia, espresso*; from Spanish *ranch, canyon, loco*; and of course many words from Ireland and Scotland as well.

Activity 3.2 Find out the origin of these words: *buccaneer, dunk, porch, piccaninny, banjo, calumet, hamburger, peccadillo, coleslaw.*[2]

Through its economic and military power American influence has increased enormously in the world, to such an extent that English, in its British and in its American variety, has ousted French as the lingua franca of diplomacy. It has increasingly become the language of industry and trade, academic discussion, and of course aviation, shipping and tourism.

Other native Englishes

Many countries in the world contribute more or less directly to the language called English. This is true of the West Indies, Australia and New Zealand, South Africa, West and East Africa, India, Pakistan, Malaysia, the Philippines, to name only a few. Often their contribution is direct, in the sense that words and phrases, perhaps borrowed from a native population to describe features of the environment, find their way into the language. Sometimes the contribution is indirect, in that a novelist describes a cultural environment, unfamiliar to the Western experience, in which a local variant of the English language is clearly the vehicle of communication.

The influence of English is felt in large areas of the modern world. In virtually all the former British colonies English has remained the language of administration, justice and education. In the Pacific British and American influence exist side by side. Former British colonies use British English, whereas most of the smaller Pacific islands including the Philippines and Formosa have generally adopted the American variety as a model.

Activity 3.3 Study the following text from VS Naipaul's novel *The Suffrage of Elvira* (Penguin 1969, p119). What grammatical features strike you as different from standard British English in the spoken form?

> **'Ah,' Baksh said heavily to Foam and Herbert. 'Campaign manager and little mister man. Where you was out so late? I did tell you to put away the dog or I did tell you to build a mansion for it?'**
>
> **Herbert smiled. 'We was out campaigning.' He winked at Foam.**
>
> **'That prove what I was saying about the elections, ma'am,' Teacher Francis said to Mrs Baksh. 'A little boy like Herbert ain't have no right to go out campaigning.'**
>
> **Mrs Baksh was on her best behaviour for the teacher. 'Is what I does forever always keep on telling the father, Teach. Beg pardon, Teach.' She**

turned to the boys. 'All your food take out and waiting for all-you in the kitchen. It must be cold as dog nose now.'[3]

Particularly since the second world war the influence of English has grown tremendously. The language of diplomacy used to be French, but with the decision to establish the main base of the United Nations in New York French influence has dwindled. Also the tendency to publish academic papers in English rather than in one's native language has given the language extra prestige.

The choice of the continued use of English in the former colonies to some extent goes back to its use in colonial times. Quite often after gaining independence there was a total lack of agreement on which of the local languages should become the standard language and therefore it was often agreed to go on using English for the business of governing the country, thus continuing existing custom.

The existence of so many different native varieties of English and the use of English for international communication may well, in the course of time, lead to a model of English which is recognizable as English but not really spoken as a native language in any specific country. Whether this comes about is as yet still uncertain. But already many non-native speakers of English in the Western world these days use a variety of English that is neither American nor British, but something in between: Mid-Atlantic. For the moment, however, English is the second language for a great many people, particularly in western Europe, but in Asia as well. This does mean that language teachers have to make up their minds about what model of English to adopt for teaching purposes.

Activity 3.4 What model of English is used for the teaching of English in your country? Do learners on the whole accept this model? What arguments are generally put forward for, or against, a British model or an American model? Are there any changes in the wind?[4]

The native varieties of British English are not as prestigious as RP or Standard British English in western Europe. But if the language is taught for international communication, varieties of spoken English must be available in the classroom illustrating versions of native use and usage, and also many non-native types of English

English as a lingua franca

The preceding sections have made at least one thing clear: the English language has assimilated a great deal of foreign influence. John Lyons (1981 pp328–9) puts it like this:

(...) English and the other major languages of Europe (...) are, in many respects, highly unrepresentative of the languages of the world. English, in particular, has been used in the administration of an empire of great cultural diversity. It is spoken as a native language by members of many different ethnic groups and adherents of many religions, living in various parts of the world. It is widely employed by anthropologists, missionaries and writers of all kinds, not only in the description of every known society, but also in novels, plays, etc, which have their setting in countries and

societies in which English is not normally spoken. This means that English, to an even greater extent than other European languages, has been enlarged and modified by loan-translation in almost every area of its vocabulary. The correlations between the semantic structure of English and the cultures of its native speakers are therefore much more complex and diverse than are the correlations between language and culture in the vast majority of human societies.

The conclusion is inescapable: if one wants to see the world and make a career, one needs English. Indeed, English is already the language of air and sea travel, and to a large extent of tourism. These days no hotel manager worthy of the name can manage without English (alongside the local language, of course). The same is true of many other registers: pop culture, computer science, but also banking, diplomacy and scholarship. English is the language of technology and commerce in the widest sense, which indicates a type of language use less influenced by national culture, but more by the culture of the specific register.

As a starting point one must speak the language of the specific subculture, if one wishes to pass as a member of the group. But much more important is adherence to and knowledge of the norms and values of the specific culture to be accepted. One shows that one belongs by obeying the unwritten rules on the way one is supposed to be dressed, the type of preferred transport, adherence to rules of behaviour and lifestyle, which may not be generally accepted within society but are certainly not wholly condemned.

Pop culture in a sense is a reaction to the dominant adult culture. For this reason, those attending pop concerts and other exhibitions of youth culture will perceive and interpret the world in terms of the values and beliefs of this subculture. The same is true, in a way, of the culture of the world of diplomacy, except that here the reaction is not so much against the dominant adult culture: it *is* the dominant adult culture. At least, the members of the diplomatic service would like to believe that they are setting the norms and values according to which the international exchange of ideas on national rights and wrongs should take place.

At the same time, particularly in an international setting, each of the participants in such subcultural meetings brings his/her own unique personality into the proceedings. Depending on one's own and one's interlocutor's notions of power distance, individuality, assertivity and tolerance of ambiguity (see Chapter 2), fed by each participant's home culture, the meeting will proceed and move towards a conclusion. Mostly the language used in such meetings, particularly when participants are from different national backgrounds, will be English. But it may well be a kind of English that owes more to its function as a 'shared means of communication' than as a language used in a specific part of the world (cf. van Essen 1991).

Form or function

Before foreign languages gained entry into the school curricula for secondary education, they were mainly taught for what now would be called 'specific purposes'. Before 1800 English was much in demand in the main ports of Europe, obviously for trading purposes. In textbooks for the Low Dutch market 'dating from this period commercial information and business letters were invariably included, but there is hardly any sign of cultural or literary interest, as was the case in the French and German-speaking areas.' (Van Essen 1991 p7)

When modern languages were introduced into the school curriculum in the 19th century, they were taught in the same way as the classical languages: through the grammar-translation method. Its main concern was with written texts. Teachers were concerned with making their learners adhere strictly to the rules of English grammar in the production of written sentences. That learners might wish to use this language in written or spoken communication never seemed to cross their minds, although there always were a few non-conformists who insisted that language was a tool for communication. The emphasis was on the written forms of the language for the simple reason that most contacts with the foreign language were in the written medium. This approach derives from the 'Age of Reason', when it was discovered that there is a distinction between *intuitive thinking* and *logical thinking*. Psychologists are rediscovering intuitive thinking as the way the human brain solves problems, using logical thinking to analyse and account for the viability of the solution found.

The demand for learning/teaching the spoken forms of the foreign language grew when the number of personal contacts between members of the trading profession and private citizens in Europe increased through improved rail and ship transport facilities in the second half of the century. The protagonists of the reform movement worked hard to develop methodology and didactics to meet the growing demand for learning the spoken language. It was a reaction against the 'what' of FLT (foreign language teaching), by an attempt to improve the 'how' (cf. Van Els *et al.* 1984 p148). Wilhelm Viètor in Germany, François Gouin in France, Henry Sweet in England, to mention only a few names, all contributed in their way to an approach to teaching and learning a foreign language which placed the main emphasis on the development of oral skills, without neglecting the written form.

The struggle between the protagonists of (grammatical) 'form' on the one hand and the adherents of (communicative) 'function' on the other has held the attention of the profession until the present. Occasionally pleas were made for an 'eclectic' approach, but the basic issue remained: 'Do we teach our learners how to analyse the language?' or 'Do we teach our learners to use the language effectively?'

Activity 3.5 How important is the teaching of grammar in your opinion? Does this agree with the time you spend on it in class? Any explanation, in case of a discrepancy?[5]

Describing a basic level of language command

It was really only during the 1960s that language teachers gradually began to resolve the form/function issue. Slowly, the idea gained ground that you learnt a language for communication with other people. The process was accelerated by the Council of Ministers of Education of the Council of Europe. The Ministers realized that with the growing integration of Europe it would be necessary to establish a system of mutual recognition of diplomas which would make it possible for the people of western Europe to move from one country to another, from one job to another, without loss of income. An integral part of this system had to be, inevitably, an accreditation scheme for the description of levels of command of foreign languages (cf. Council of Europe 1973).

A working group of experts, chaired by the British scholar John Trim, was asked to develop a unit-credit system for language learning in Europe. The first task the group was set was to produce a description of a minimum requirement of mastery of a language, termed the 'threshold level', which would make it possible for someone who had achieved this level to survive in the foreign country. A Dutchman, Dr JA van Ek, was invited to describe this level for English. His work was published in 1975, and was soon followed by similar descriptions for German, French, Spanish and other languages of member states of the Council of Europe. Now the list of published threshold level descriptions covers virtually all the languages including Maltese, Basque, Dutch, Letzebürgisch (the native language of Luxemburg) and many other languages.

Activity 3.6 Levels of mastery of another language cannot be defined in terms of mastery of its rules of grammar. There is more to using a language than just the correct application of its grammatical rules. How would you go about defining different levels of mastery of English? What aspects of language use should find a place in the different level descriptions?[6]

This was the problem to be solved by the members of Trim's working group. After due deliberation they decided that a threshold level could perhaps be best defined as the level necessary for survival as a tourist visiting another country. The idea was that as a tourist you have certain minimum requirements, like somewhere to sleep, something to eat, ways of finding your way about in the country, and so on. You also need to know something about the law and certain customs of the country you are visiting: simple things like traffic regulations and passport and visa requirements.

The next step was then to draw up as complete a list of language situations (settings) as possible and to make inventories of words and idioms and grammatical structures needed to function adequately in certain social and psychological roles in these settings.

Activity 3.7 Make a list of the settings you might have to cope with as a visitor to another country. You could start as follows: at the customs, traffic regulations, reporting lost property at the police station. ... Compare your list with Van Ek's survey (in *Systems Development in Adult Language Learning*, Council of Europe 1973 p103). Was your list different from Van Ek's? Was it an improvement on the original? What would be the use of such a list and the accompanying analysis of its grammatical structures and vocabulary for the language learning situation?[7]

A new syllabus

The Threshold Level (Van Ek 1975), which superseded the first draft in Section 2, Part 3 of *Systems Development in Adult Language Learning* (Council of Europe 1973), caused a tremendous stir in the world of foreign language syllabus design. Up to the time of its publication textbook materials were organized on the basis of a list of grammatical structures ordered according to the 'best' way of presenting them. Suddenly this list was relegated to second or perhaps even third place on the order of priorities. Now textbooks began a unit with a dialogue illustrating language use in a particular setting, followed by exercises drilling the learner in the use of specific forms of language.

Many teachers felt at a loss, until they discovered that textbooks organized according to settings and notions and functions still had to refer to grammatical distinctions and differences between mother tongue and second language. 'By 1970 language teaching experts were keenly aware of the loss of direction and the confusion among teachers that had ensued. For quite a few teachers the turmoil and the disorientation signalled a partial return to the old routine of the grammar-translation method, the only difference being that a teaching unit no longer began with a rule of grammar but with a dialogue, that translations were out and that they had been replaced by structural drill in written form.' (Van Essen 1989a p8)

It took some years for the experts to discover ways of dealing with the new demands of language teaching. In Germany Edelhoff edited a collection of studies dealing with the principles underlying a communicative approach to the teaching of English and offering an exercise typology which was intended to build up the learner's confidence in going from 'organizing information' to 'using skills' (*Bundesarbeitsgemeinschaft Englisch an Gesamtschulen* 1978). This study was translated into English by Candlin (1981). At about the same time a similar study appeared for the teaching of German (Neuner, Krüger, Grewer 1981). The communicative approach slowly found its way into EFL textbooks.

Activity 3.8 Make a comparison of a textbook for EFL (English as a foreign language) published at a time just after the introduction of threshold level-type requirements for foreign languages and a recent one. What is different in the organization of the material, the selection of texts and exercise types, and the tests supplied by the authors to check on the progress made by the learners?[8]

Teaching discourse

Changes came about gradually. The problem that could only be mastered in time was that language teaching experts knew so little about the system of rules underlying spoken and written discourse. One such difficulty is that a speaker sometimes uses a phrase in a sense which is completely different from its normal meaning, or a phrase that conveys its message in an indirect way. A phrase like: 'It's my turn to walk the dog tonight' acquires its real meaning when it is recognized as a reply to, for example, 'How about going out for a drink?' A more conventional way of declining the invitation could have been: 'I'm terribly sorry', which is an indirect way of saying the conventional: 'No, I can't'. But then, knowing that speakers obviously use their language in this way is not enough to tell you when it is allowable to use unconventional phrases or indirect speech acts. Even the knowledge that the option depends on the awareness that speaker and hearer share a certain amount of knowledge of setting, topic, roles, language and culture is perhaps not enough for most learners.

Fortunately, context often provides clues to the interpretation of particular utterances. For example, when a mother asks her child: 'Would you like to read this story?', holding out a book, the child knows that it is being offered a choice. This is not true when the same phrase is used in the language classroom: the child has no choice but to read the story, probably only a few sentences, and aloud. This quite common phenomenon did not appear in the original *Threshold Level* (see Willems and De Jong 1989). In the second version of Van Ek's study this omission has been rectified (Van Ek and Trim 1991). This appeared fifteen years after the first *Threshold Level.*

Activity 3.9 Make a list of (in)direct phrases for a function such as: to promise, to apologize, to reject an offer, to thank, to excuse, to agree/disagree, both for your own language and for English. Most of your phrases will probably be conventional. Can you think of any unconventional ways of saying these things, again in both languages? Can you discover correspondences?[9]

Developments in the field of discourse must find their way into EFL materials and the language class. One problem is that in the classroom much language use is 'transactional', ie intended to get things done, whereas outside the classroom 'interactional' use of language occurs frequently. 'Interactional talk ... has as its primary functions the lubrication of the social wheels, establishing roles and relationships with another person prior to transactional talk, confirming and consolidating relationships, expressing solidarity, and so on' (McCarthy 1991 p136).

Probably the most effective way of helping learners to become aware of how strategies for opening and closing a discourse, turn-taking conventions, etc, may differ from one culture to another is through exposure to authentic extracts of spoken discourse and focusing on language and strategies used by interactants afterwards.

Objectives for language learning

Objectives for the teaching and learning of foreign languages have been around for some years now. In the 1960s a national curriculum was circulated in the Netherlands. It stated in general terms what was expected from the learners after three or five/six years of language learning in secondary education. These aims were formulated in terms of degrees of correctness of application of rules of grammar, pronunciation and vocabulary use. Apart from this, learners were also expected to be knowledgeable, to some extent, about the literary canon of the foreign language concerned in order to gain some understanding of the foreign culture. A translation into English of Section I reads as follows:

> *General*
> **In the curriculum two phases are distinguished:**
> **1 the basic programme in the first three years of pre-university ('*vwo*') and higher general education ('*havo*') and the four years of more general education ('*mavo*');**
> **2 education in the two final years of higher general education and the final three years of pre-university education.**
> ***During the first phase* learners must learn to understand, to speak, to read and to write. At the same time they must acquire some knowledge of the people and the culture of the country discussed.**
> ***During the second phase* the teaching is organized thus that the learners maintain and gain better control of the basic techniques, that they, also individually, become acquainted with spoken and written linguistic utterances of the other people and in this way gain more in-depth knowledge of the culture of this people.**
> **(*Voorstel Leerplan rijksscholen voor vwo/havo/mavo*, Ministerie van Onderwijs en Wetenschappen, Den Haag 1968, author's translation)**

The definition of 'culture' remains rather unclear. There is no mention of it in the statements relevant to *phase one*, but there is an implied relationship with literary products in the specifications for *phase two*:

> **The curriculum for *the second phase* comprises: *A* Extension of the skill achieved in understanding, speaking, reading and writing; *B* Listening to, reading, interpreting and summarizing of literary and other linguistic utterances; *C* The reading of literary works, on the basis of which insight into and knowledge of literature is taught.'**
> **(Ibid.)**

Objectives such as these express '... a relationship between learning to read and write a language and studying literature, philosophy, science produced by individuals in societies which spoke the language or at least used it for recording its achievements.' (Byram and Esarte-Sarries 1991 p3). With hindsight such objectives contradict what most people today feel to be acceptable aims for the learning and teaching of languages.

Activity 3.10 Why did you wish to study and learn English? Did your objective at the time agree with any official statement of objectives for learning English in your country?[10]

Seen in historical perspective it is clear why it was felt to be necessary to insist on knowing the grammar, vocabulary, idioms and literature of the foreign language. It was not until the last quarter of the last century, and the beginning of the twentieth century, that it became possible to study modern languages at Dutch universities, in line with developments in most other western European countries. In order to prove themselves a worthy partner in the corridors of academe, university lecturers and professors had to prove themselves academically respectable. This they did through the study of the evolution of language: its historical grammar. To some extent this was a respectable activity, since it went back to the historical precedents of Latin, and the much older Sanskrit. Alongside grammar, the study of literature also was given a chance to prove itself.

Objectives for all school subjects are traditionally derived from the academic discipline. This sometimes led to somewhat curious exam requirements. Just one example will have to do: in the Dutch school system it was customary to require from the learners that they read a certain number of literary works reflecting historical literary developments. For pre-university secondary education this might be as many as twelve to fifteen titles. For the level just below this it was usual to require eight to ten titles. For the lowest level of general education five or six and for pupils who could not cope with a general secondary education, but attended phase one of vocational education, the requirement was three or four. In practice, of course, few teachers insisted on the literary status of the titles on the reading list, particularly at the lower levels, but the requirement does show what people felt was a suitable reflection of language learning objectives.

Activity 3.11 What are the reading requirements for English in your country for the various levels of secondary education? Are they the same for mother tongue and foreign languages? Is the difference one of quantity or of quality?[11]

Objectives are a statement of goals, that is, they are a formulation of what an individual learner wishes/needs to achieve in a course of education in a particular subject. It is a matter of either/or. On the one hand there are the providers of educational facilities: the state, a firm, a private institution. On the other there are the learners' private ambitions, their goals in life. Generally learners will find it very difficult to be explicit about why they wish to learn English. Quite often they have no alternative but to rely on claims stated about a course, made by the providers.

Activity 3.12 What does a language teacher need to know for a teaching qualification in English as a foreign language, and what levels of mastery would he/she need to command for a career? What types of text should he/she be able to read; what types of text should he/she be able to write; what varieties of English must he/she be able to deal with in oral interaction; and what level of correctness and appropriacy in language use does he/she need for oral presentation in class, and at seminars and conferences (with colleagues)?[12]

Objectives and testing

You must have found the last activity quite difficult. It comes as no surprise therefore that many learners find this type of activity terrifying. All the same they are usually quite firm about what it is they want to learn and what not. The problem is, they may not have the language, even in their mother tongue, to formulate what they intuitively 'know'. It is quite an achievement already for them to have realized they need to know English for their career.

Fortunately there are many types of statements of objectives available. Most countries specify school-leaving exam requirements for their educational systems. Sometimes there is a prescribed set syllabus to work through as well. Examples of exam papers may be available to check on how achievement is evaluated. The same is true of internationally accepted qualifications such as the TOEFL (the Test Of English as a Foreign Language) or the Cambridge Certificate of Proficiency. Private language schools have found it necessary to be very explicit about the levels their students have mastered, since claiming too much for the quality of their training programmes would be disastrous.

The following is the description of Level 3 of the English Speaking Union's Nine-Level Scale:

> **Uses a limited range of language, sufficient for simple practical needs. In more exacting situations, there are frequent problems in accuracy, fluency, appropriacy and organization, so that normal communication and comprehension frequently break down or are difficult to keep going.**

Such statements are not very helpful to outsiders, unless they are accompanied by an operationalization. Insiders on the whole find working with formulas such as these not too difficult.

Activity 3.13 What is to be understood by 'a limited range of language', 'simple practical needs', 'more exacting situations'? In other words: how would you operationalize these notions? Give topics, and associated functions and notions. How would you define 'problems in accuracy, fluency, appropriacy, and organization'? Give examples of each of these from your own experience or from what you have heard or seen from others' use of English as a foreign language.[13]

Even though the wish to be precise in this type of statement is present, in practice a combination of test results and intuitive assessment on the part of an experienced examiner often prove necessary. The difficulty often appears to be of two kinds: the author of the statement is generally an expert in the field and tries to be as explicit as he/she possibly can, but the practising teacher, lacking the required level of expertise, does not understand the statement in quite the way the author had in mind. Secondly, the teacher's main focus is on classroom procedures, getting the learners to learn as much as they can from the materials provided, and statements of objectives in this setting are of secondary importance, additionally because the textbook is expected to achieve them anyway.

Testing serves various functions. Placement tests, for instance, such as are used for example in private education, serve the function of assessing a learner's ability to attend classes in the particular range of subjects. For English, as for other languages, such assessments tend to test only those aspects of language mastery the school, or rather the English department, normally tests: communicative ability or just grammatical ability and vocabulary knowledge, or whatever combination of skills and knowledge happens to be favoured.

Schools usually find it necessary to check on the progress made by learners, in order to be able to decide 'objectively' whether a learner has managed to gain enough knowledge for entry into and a fair chance to pass through the next level. Such objectives will be stated in the school curriculum, if all is well. Testing these is left to the department. If the educational organization of the country arranges school-leaving examinations, the exam papers will probably be provided by an independent state-supervised organization. This type of paper will undoubtedly influence the language department as to the type of tests they will set their learners. Some countries prefer university entrance examinations, ie exams developed, set and assessed by individual universities.

The field of language teaching objectives and their evaluation apparently shares many of the characteristics of a minefield. Superficially everything is quite clear and safe, but it is probably inherent in the nature of language that language teachers are seldom happy with the testing formats they are expected to use to assess the level of language mastery their learners have achieved. 'Handle testing with care' is probably the best advice one can give, and particularly 'Never assume that the definitive test format for measuring language mastery is available'.

At present the most favourable assessment of the testing problem seems to be that the measurement of skills and subskills using properly validated objective test instruments only provides us with part of the answers we want. It is better to translate our objectives into a series of tasks, each requiring integrated bits of the original objectives.

Activity 3.14 A simple language learning objective is that learners should be able to give personal information. Devise three or four different settings in which one may be required to give personal information, and draw up a set of roleplay instructions accordingly.[14]

Objectives have to be clear to those involved in the course, teachers as well as learners. The aims of a particular course of language teaching therefore need to be explained to the learners taking the course. Thus, everybody will know what all the effort is intended to achieve.

A statement of objectives, however, is not the same thing as a statement of the methodology to be used. Objectives state the desired behaviour of learners at the end of the course; the way in which they may be achieved is a different matter. This issue will receive due attention in the final chapter where methodology is discussed. Here I will just state that there must be a relationship between the means used to achieve the learners' objectives and learner motivation. In simple words, if you know why you are doing certain things, it is much easier to go on doing them, even when you don't particularly enjoy doing them.

Influenced by the ideas presented by the group of experts working under the aegis of the Cultural Council of the Council of Europe, to give it its proper reference, massive reconsideration of language learning objectives has taken place in the countries of western Europe. The results all follow the lead given in the *Threshold Level.* The *Hessische Rahmenrichtlinien* were probably the earliest spin-off, and the Dutch *Advies kerndoelen voor de basisvorming in basisonderwijs en voortgezet onderwijs* ('Advice core-objectives for basic education in primary and secondary education') (Ministerie van Onderwijs en Wetenschappen, Zoetermeer 1989, author's translation) for modern language learning may well be the latest but not the last. All such publications show a concern with the practical application of what is learnt in the foreign language class in everyday contexts requiring the use of the foreign language.

Activity 3.15 Study the section on modern languages in the latest publication of modern language learning objectives for phase 1 of secondary education in your country, making a list of the settings mentioned for oral communication. Compare this list with that in the latest Threshold Level publication. Can you account for the differences?[15]

The change in attitude to language learning objectives, no longer a straight derivation from what the academic discipline requires, but a visible concern with the needs of the learner, has also led to a different attitude to the methodology and didactics of teaching foreign languages. Putting the learner's needs in the central position led to the Council of Europe's group of experts (Trim 1985) asking some very pertinent questions, such as: who decides on the exact objectives for learning foreign languages (the learner or ...?); who decides on the most suitable learning activities (the learner or ...?); who plans the learner's progress towards the goals (the teacher or ...?).

Activity 3.16 What is your opinion on these three questions: Who decides on the exact objectives for learning foreign languages? Who decides on the most suitable learning activities? Who plans the learner's progress towards the goals?[16]

From teaching to learning

Over the centuries good teachers have always managed to persuade their learners that it would be good and useful for them to learn what they were being offered. Focusing slightly differently, good teachers generally arouse the interest of their pupils sufficiently so that they (the pupils) take the learning task into their own hands and only look for guidance and help from their teacher when they meet an insoluble problem. This was also recognized by the Council of Europe's group of experts. They made an inventory of experiments set up to push learner autonomy, that is, to make the learner responsible for organizing his/her own curriculum, learning activities and evaluation (Holec 1988). Holec's collection shows convincingly that stimulating and developing learner autonomy works in all the cultural settings where this has been tried out. It works with young children and adults; it works in state-supervised education and in private institutions; and it works in all the countries in which it has been tried.

In a small-scale publication entitled *Proposals for National Criteria Modern Languages in the First Phase of Secondary Education: General Objectives and Concrete Core Objectives* (Galjee 1989) we find seven core objectives. The first one states in general terms what is expected of the learner in a number of communication situations – to be specified later in the text in the 'concrete core objectives' – where the foreign language must be used. There then follow three objectives dealing with the learner's contribution to the learning process: the development of strategies to cope with texts, gaining experience with extensive reading, and acquiring compensatory strategies to understand and/or produce texts. Objectives 5 and 6 are concerned with the foreign language as spoken in its native environment and used in international communication, and with its relationship to culture. The final objective deals with the idea of learner autonomy and is worth quoting in full:

> **The learners can relate the learning of foreign languages to their own needs and experiences. Particularly:**
> **– they have some insight into the objectives set to them and/or into those they might choose for themselves;**
> **– they have some familiarity with procedures and aids which will contribute to the achievement of these objectives;**
> **– they are capable of assessing, in ways appropriate to their own ends, their progress in foreign language acquisition.**
> **(Ibid. p4)**

The idea that learners are invited to assess their own progress is bound to cause some consternation in many traditional classrooms. All the same, it is at least a notion worth thinking through in all its consequences (cf. Council of Europe 1988, and in particular the contribution to this publication by Mats Oskarsson); certainly, when we realize that it has been tried with learners of all ages and in all types of education, and that it has been shown to work, moreover, that most learners actually prefer to be responsible for their own learning, rather than be told what to do. In Chapters 4 and 5 this area will be discussed in more detail.

The definition of (socio-)cultural competence

In the formulation of objectives for foreign language learning it has become quite common to find reference to knowledge of and familiarity with cultural norms and values, and also competence in dealing with social rituals that are different in the native language. The reason for explicit mention of objectives for encounters with members of other cultures whose native language is English or who use English as a lingua franca is simply that interaction involves more than correct use of grammatical and idiomatic rules.

In person-to-person contacts facial expression, tone, body movements are at least as important as the actual words spoken. And these words have, besides, to fit appropriately into the context of use. *The Threshold Level 1990* puts it like this:

> **In using English for professional purposes, no less than for any other purpose, people will have to be able to ask questions and to provide information, to elicit opinions, views, preferences, and to express them, to refer to past, present and future events, to express reasons why and conditions under which something may come to pass and to understand others doing so, etc. Also, they will have to be familiar with certain social conventions and common assumptions inherent in manners of expression in the English language, and they will need to be aware of how cultural differences may be reflected in communicative behaviour. And then, of course, they will also need experience in coping with the inevitable occurrence of situations which overtax their linguistic or sociocultural resources.**
> **(Van Ek and Trim, 1991 p3)**

Activity 3.17 *The Threshold Level 1990* offers the following objective in the context of Social Conventions and Rituals:

> 2 *Visiting rituals*
> **The learners know – or can inquire:**
> **– whether they are expected to be punctual;**
> **– whether they are expected to bring a present, and if so what sort of present;**
> **– what sort of clothes to wear;**
> **– whether to expect refreshments, or a meal, if asked for a certain time;**
> **– whether, and how, they are expected to comment on food, furnishings, etc;**
> **– how long they are expected to stay as well as when and how to take leave.**
> **(Ibid. p104)**

Check with an EFL textbook whether this type of problem is dealt with, in what manner and how fully. If the outcome is negative, how would you deal with the problem?[17]

Clearly this type of objective applies in contacts between native speakers and foreigners, but also in lingua franca situations. It refers to knowledge of the world that may not be readily available to every learner, although some may in fact be familiar with it. In the next two chapters methodological insights and pedagogic ideas will be discussed more fully.

Notes

1 The EEC treaty of 1957 guarantees the free movement of persons, employees and professionals, and their right to work throughout the Community. Foreign employees and professionals have the same rights as residents, which means that they must receive equal treatment regarding such issues as pay, social security, tax, union membership, housing. To facilitate the establishment of professionals throughout the Community, member states have to recognize diplomas from other states. For some professions a lot of progress has been made, but not for all. When one feels discriminated against on the grounds of nationality, the European Court in Luxembourg can be asked to give a verdict, which will always overrule the law of the country concerned.

2 Any good dictionary should supply the information which I found in the *Shorter Oxford English Dictionary*, third revised edition, of 1966. This type of exercise is useful to do with students, of course. Words may be selected from Australian, New Zealand, Indian, South African English for a start. Many dictionaries provide etymological information, ie information on the origin and history of a word or phrase. One helpful source may be Eric Partridge, *Origins, A Short Etymological Dictionary of Modern English*, Book Club Associates 1978. More recent is *The Dictionary of English Language and Culture*, Longman 1992. This dictionary provides cultural notes on usage for many words and phrases.

3 This activity is particularly useful for students to do. It teaches them the relative value of traditional grammar and that much of what they have had to learn in the field of morphology concerns rules that apply to mainly Standard British English, and hardly at all to other varieties.

4 If we decide to teach English for international communication, we must bear in mind how its native speakers use the language. However, there are many groups of native speakers, each with their own ways of using the opportunities offered by the language. You only have to think of the way English is spoken in the United States, Northern Ireland, Australia, Kenya, Jamaica, Nigeria, India and Pakistan, and so on. Sometimes mutual understanding is hindered by the fact that the speakers use the same language. Just ask an Englishman and an American where you would find 'the office on the second floor'. You would find the American sending you up one flight of stairs and the Englishman needing two.

In western Europe tradition favours British RP, although today this is mostly watered down to Standard British English. Occasionally one comes across references to Mid-Atlantic, a variety acceptable to speakers from either side of the Atlantic although native to neither.

5 Research indicates that adults profit from explanation of the system of grammatical description. Younger learners are hardly interested in the theory of grammar. They will learn a rule, though, when they have discovered that a particular grammatical error leads to misunderstandings, as in: 'He lived in London for some time', when the intention was: 'He has lived in London for some time'. The difference in meaning was realized when the interlocutor asked 'Oh, when did he leave? I thought he was still living there.'

6 The traditional distinction of the four skills is not on the whole very helpful, as it is not concerned with the communicative function of language. Much more useful is a typology at present being discussed by a working group of the Council of Europe. It distinguishes four types of communicative activity with subactivities: 'comprehension', with subactivities viewing, listening, reading, where communication is in one direction; 'interaction', with subactivities transactions, conversation (informal), discussion (formal), where communication is bi-directional; 'production', with subactivities presentations (spoken), letters, reports (written), where communication again is in one direction (away from the speaker); and 'processing', with subactivities listening and note taking, reading and synthesizing, interpreting (spoken, informal), translating (written, formal), where communication goes both ways again. This model makes it possible to link language activities to specific settings which may be ordered according to the difficulty of the language that will be used in that setting, eg in terms of in/formality, complexity of discourse, etc.

7 It proved possible to describe an even lower stage of survival English: JA van Ek, LG Alexander and MA Fitzpatrick, *Waystage English*, Pergamon Press 1977. Dr JA van Ek also wrote a version specifically for secondary education: *The Threshold Level for Modern Language Learning in Schools*, Wolters Noordhoff Longman, Groningen, the Netherlands 1976. To some extent the discrepancies may be explained in terms of the public you had in mind.

McCarthy has this to say:

Spoken discourse types can be analysed for their typical patterns and the linguistic realizations that accompany them (eg service encounters, business negotiations, telephone calls, chat-show interviews, lectures, trouble-sharing encounters, etc), and the periodical literature of

discourse analysis abounds in detailed studies of a vast range of types. These studies are most often not carried out with any overt pedagogical aim, but are very useful for language teachers and materials writers who want to create systematic speaking skills programmes and whose goal is to design activities that will generate output as close as possible to naturally occurring talk. Complete naturalness is probably impossible in the classroom, but the feeling of engaging in an authentic activity is important to the learner, as is the feeling of being taught authentic and naturally occurring structures and vocabulary to use in simulations of real-life talk.

(McCarthy 1991 pp144–5)

8 Hopefully you found that texts in the more recent textbook were more authentic, that there was a wider range of exercises following the A, B, C, D model of Candlin (1981), and that tests were of integrated skills and not just of grammar and vocabulary.

9 It is often in this area that foreigners make errors by producing phrases that are literal translations of things they would say in their own language, like the Dutch lady offering another cup of coffee to her British guest, saying 'I still have some coffee.' Her guest found it very hard to understand that she was being offered another cup of coffee, understandably, since this phrase meant something completely different to her. (Willems, in H van Dijck, ed. 1991)

10 From informal contacts I have come to realize that my own experience is fairly common. I was interested in English and found that studying this language had very little to do with what I wanted to know about the country, its history, its culture, etc. Fortunately I found that I shared this interest with some of my teachers at the university. So I stayed on.

11 Proposals for changes in the final exam requirements for phase two of secondary education in the Netherlands do away with the literary canon to a large extent. Reading remains important, but the requirement of familiarity with different text types has become more important than familiarity with the foreign language's literary history. A special option, 'European culture and literature', will be available for those pupils who have taken an interest in this subject. They will be confronted with publications in English, French and German, and/or translations of these in Dutch.

12 *Attainment Targets for Foreign Language Teacher Education in Europe* (GM Willems ed., Brussels 1993) has the following to say about the future teacher's foreign language competencies:

Foreign language teachers have:

... acquired a *pronunciation*, both segmental and suprasegmental, of the standard dialect of the target language which makes them easy to understand and enables them to understand with ease other speakers of a standard variant of the target language. Although a slight colouring of their target language pronunciation by mother-tongue setting, and of its communicative use by prosodic conventions of the mother tongue is permissible, this colouring should not lead to recurrent communication problems in interactions with native and fluent non-native speakers of the target language; (...)

... developed *conversational skills* to the extent that they can serve as models for their learners and that they can communicate with native and non-native speakers of the target language with ease on topics that may be considered to lie within their sphere of interest as professionals. Their *strategic use of language functions and repertoire of discourse regulatory formulas* approach that of the native speaker. The use of *compensatory strategies* when their linguistic or pragmatic ('declarative') competence lets them down deserves special mention under this heading as forming part and parcel of exo-linguistic communication (communication in which at least one of the interactants is not using his/her mother-tongue);

... acquired a *vocabulary* in the target language on topics that may be considered to lie within their professional sphere of interest;

... acquired an elementary insight into *pragmatics*. They understand 'how to do things with words' ie on the one hand how to realize functions in the target language (both in indirect and unconventional ways and in direct and conventional ways) and on the other how to open, close and regulate discourse, by contrasting foreign language conventions with their mother-tongue conventions on the basis of an elementary insight into *discourse analysis*; they also understand how compensatory strategies form an integral part of any communication in which negotiation of meaning is the issue;

... a basic awareness and understanding of how the *sociocultural embeddedness of the target language manifests itself* in the way the language is used for communication;

... acquired communicative skills in the foreign language in which there are *no recurrent grammatical errors*; (...)

... developed sufficient *listening skills* to

enable them to follow and comprehend with ease generally accepted variants of the target language, spoken at normal rate, on topics and in situations that belong to their professional sphere of interest (both interactionally/transactionally and unilaterally: lectures, talks); (...)

... developed sufficient *reading skills* to be able to read with ease texts in the target language aimed at the general educated reader and texts concerning their didactic and methodological practice; (...)

... developed *writing skills* that enable them to write a personal letter, a business letter, summaries, reports and modest literary products, observing target language conventions (linear, concentric, digressive etc); (...)

... are skilled in speaking to groups demonstrating clear diction, imaginative openness and the will to be creative;

... are skilled in adapting their communicative competence in classroom management, in giving instructions and explanations matched to the level of proficiency of their learners; they know when it is wise to shift to the use of a shared mother-tongue (in case there is one) to facilitate explanations, negotiation and theory building.
(pp41–3)

13 This activity can be very useful for students to do particularly if a selection of exam formats is available which they can then assign to a particular specification. Basically, intuition inspired by experience helps the language teacher to overcome the difficulty of unclear phrasing in this type of document. A useful follow-up, of course, is to organize the list of topics, language functions and notions into a mini-syllabus.

14 Settings might be: booking a place at a camp site; reporting lost property at a railway station/police station; being interviewed as a witness of an accident; arriving at a training institute for a language course; etc. Depending on the level of 'world knowledge' of the learners the role of interviewer is made more or less explicit as to what questions to ask and what information to gather. The other role simply supplies relevant (personal) information.

These days a new language is learnt for use in communication. Hence, in the course of learning it, learners will wish to try out what they have learnt so far. This almost inevitably leads to learning activities which involve the learners in communication in the foreign language in a non-threatening context. I would suggest therefore that the result of this activity and similar ones be used in class for the learners (of an appropriate level) to find out if they can fulfil the requirement at some future moment.

15 If there are any big differences, it is likely that they are caused by the type of learner for whom these objectives are intended. Van Ek's *Threshold Level* (Strasbourg 1975) was for adults. Younger learners, as indicated above, have somewhat different requirements.

16 Hopefully you opted for the learner. Basically motivation is the key to success. In spite of what teachers and textbooks prescribe, learners decide what it is they want to learn and apply. At the same time they often manage quite well to reproduce what is demanded for a particular test, and forget immediately afterwards what it was they needed to know, eg when they are required to learn X (bilingual) pages of vocabulary and idioms. At the same time of course the education authority, or examination board, sets objectives for a particular type of schooling, and teachers are required to select appropriate textbook materials to achieve these. The point is, what does the learner do with what he/she is set to learn? Does he/she integrate this into his/her experience, or is the bit of learning dropped immediately?

17 If the problem is dealt with in the textbook, you are fortunate. If not, you could introduce activities along these lines: find/write a text describing an incident where something went wrong, like the Dutch businessman who was invited to a Frenchman's home at 8 o'clock in the evening. The Dutchman and his wife had their dinner at six (usual time for the main hot meal of the day in the Netherlands) and arrived punctually at eight, to discover to their dismay that a full four-course dinner was waiting for them. They tried to do justice to the meal, but did not quite succeed of course. Present the text (from the Frenchman's or the Dutchman's point of view) and ask your class (1) how they would have coped with the situation and (2) what information they would have needed to avoid this problem.

Suggestions for further study

Some years ago BBC television broadcast an exciting serial called *The Story of English*. Simultaneously a book was published: Robert McCrum, William Cran and Robert McNeil, *The Story of English* (Faber & Faber and BBC Publications 1986). If you want a well presented overview of the state of English in the world, and what historical processes contributed to its influential status, I advise you to get hold of the book and video.

Several books are available dealing with the growth of English to its present importance. David Crystal, *The English Language* (Pelican Books 1988) is very informative and contains an annotated list of recent books for further study. Robert Phillipson, *Linguistic Imperialism* (Oxford University Press 1992) is concerned with English as a world language, how this position has come about and how EFL teachers have to be wary when they teach English. For the development of English outside Britain particularly there is: J Platt, H Weber and ML Ho, *The New Englishes* (Routledge and Kegan Paul 1984), and also Braj B Kachru, *The Alchemy of English* (Pergamon Press 1986). Up-to-date information can be found in back issues of *World Englishes, Journal of English as an International and Intranational Language*, Pergamon Press. At its outset in 1981 it was called *World Language English*, but changed its name on acquiring a new editor in Professor Braj B Kachru.

Publications on varieties of English as a native language are widely available, for example: Dennis R Preston and Roger W Shuy, *Varieties of American English, A Reader*, (USIS, Washington 1984), and Peter Trudgill and Jean Hannah, *International English: A Guide to Varieties of Standard English* (Edward Arnold 1982).

The history of language teaching has been told in many publications. In: Theo van Els *et al.*, *Applied Linguistics and the Learning and Teaching of Foreign Languages* (Edward Arnold 1984), a helpful survey is available, plus an overview of relevant research up to the early 1980s in the field of language learning and teaching. HH Stern, *Fundamental Concepts of Language Teaching* (Oxford University Press 1983), covers similar ground. His *Issues and Options in Language Teaching* (Oxford University Press 1992), extends the discussion of *Fundamental Concepts of Language Teaching* to actual classroom practice. H Douglas Brown, *Principles of Language Learning and Teaching* (second edition, Prentice Hall 1987) may also come in handy, particularly since he deals with the American contribution to foreign language teaching.

The latest on *Attainment Targets for Foreign Language Teacher Education in Europe, a European View* (1993), Gerard Willems (ed.), ATEE, 60, Rue de la Concorde, B 1050 Brussels, is the product of the ATEE Working Group on the Education and Training of Language Teachers. The publication discusses the requirements of the non-native teacher of modern languages from the point of view of the internationalization of education in Europe and was funded by LINGUA.

Chapter 4 The multicultural classroom and the negotiated syllabus

Direct experience of another country involves not only the cognitive but also the affective dimension of the personality. The individual needs to be able to accept and cope with ways of thinking and also modes of behaviour which are new. Furthermore his own mode of behaviour must at least be tolerated by people in the country being visited if a sense of being ill at ease is to be avoided. Language teaching becomes associated with the notion of encouraging tolerance of that which is alien and potentially threatening or unpleasant, and the instilling of behaviour which is acceptable in the foreign country.
(Michael Byram and Veronica Esarte-Sarries, *Investigating Cultural Studies in Foreign Language Teaching*, Multilingual Matters 1991 p6)

Introduction

Teaching a foreign language in the multicultural classroom involves at least two things: allowing each learner to be an autonomous person and, on the part of the teacher and the rest of the class, accepting this autonomous person. Being this kind of autonomous individual inevitably means that one accepts other people as autonomous persons as well. In a Council of Europe publication it was put like this: 'The intercultural approach means mutual recognition between cultures of origin and host cultures, and between the various cultural expressions (of the migrants and the indigenous population) in a single local community. These cultures are never static, but creative; they change according to the interactions at work.' (Rey 1986 p25) The only criticism one could level against this statement is that it treats the idea of culture as a monolithic entity that sets one country apart from another, as if the dimension of collectivity (Hofstede 1991) applies everywhere.

In the multicultural classroom representatives of different cultures will be present. Sometimes the differences will be great, but it may only be a matter of different colours of skin which sets some pupils apart from the rest of the class. Mutual recognition and acceptance of cultural differences look so obvious, but in practice prove not to be simple, for a great many reasons. In this chapter I will discuss developments towards learner autonomy and its consequences for classroom procedures concerning achieving language teaching objectives, always bearing in mind that our main concern is the multicultural classroom.

Attitudes to education

A little history

The discussion about the issues involved in dealing with different cultures in the classroom touches on attitudes to education. Historically, in most of western Europe 'learning to read and write' was the prerogative of the chosen few, which originally meant those who were being trained for the priesthood. Reserving this skill for the special caste of the priests helped to preserve the influence, power and privileges of the church.

However, people outside the priesthood, beginning with the upper classes, also desired to be able to use the tool of writing and the skill of reading for a number of purposes, mainly to preserve historic decisions and be able to refer to them if necessary. In due course the middle classes felt obliged to acquire the skills of reading and writing too. And so, gradually, the skills were allowed to spread throughout society, so that nowadays every child is taught to read and write (and to do arithmetic, of course). Being properly educated is still in many countries a privilege reserved for members of the 'better classes'. It takes energy and intelligence to break through the walls surrounding privilege.

Based on this concept of the role of education in society, the teacher's role in the teaching/learning process has for a long time been that of the dispenser of knowledge, the organizer of the teaching/learning process, the person responsible for its end product, performing this task as the representative of the ruling classes. The learner's task was much simpler. He/She had to gain entrance into this privileged institution; once in, the future was generally to a large extent assured.

Today the role of the teacher is moving towards that of 'facilitator', ie the person who helps the learning process along by providing guidance when and where needed, allowing learners to tackle problems in their own way, being present as a source of information, in short by 'managing the process' rather than by giving instruction and drill sessions.

Activity 4.1 In many countries compulsory education up to the age of about 15 offers one school curriculum for all learners. Is this a feature of the educational system in your country? If this is the case, do foreign languages figure in the curriculum and, if so, what aspects of the foreign culture are dealt with in the syllabus?[1]

Parents and the education of their children

The kind of education that parents seek for their children is traditionally related to cultural attitudes concerning power distance, attitudes to boys and girls, etc. But, as was said before, such attitudes are not generally static. Of course, when humans are very young their parents will take decisions for them. For one thing, young children are not in a position to weigh the pros and cons of a decision and therefore must often allow someone else to take it for them. As they grow up and get to know the world better, the ability to look after their own interests increases. The number of occasions when the child feels old enough to deal with matters alone will grow, which may cause a bit of strife: the age of puberty is one such time that all parents recognize.

Recently a research project in the Netherlands on the relationships between parents and children came to the conclusion that there are four types of parental behaviour towards children (reported by Yolande De Best in *Ouders van Nu*, May 1994).

Parents of type one leave their children to their own devices. As long as the child does not bother them with irrelevancies life is happy. Intrusions into the parents' peace and quiet are mostly not accepted: the child is left to fend for itself, until an emergency makes the parents' attention unavoidable. Doing things together happens only rarely in this type of family.

A second group of parents are like the first in that they do not spend too much time with their children. The main difference, however, is that these parents wish their children to become independent, autonomous, to achieve something useful in their lives. They will start things together, but very soon leave the child to fend for itself, while they do their own thing.

The traditional parents are a third group. They generally impose a code of behaviour derived from outside authority. This is mostly their religion, of whatever denomination. The child is firmly drilled to behave according to the teachings of this authority, and no misbehaviour is accepted. Sometimes the ultimate authority is Dad, and not some vague outside personality. Sometimes mother may stand in for the father, but any difficult decision will be referred to him and decided by him alone.

The final group, and the largest apparently in the Netherlands, forms a happy blend of traditional and innovative approaches to parenthood. These parents are happy to guide the child towards autonomous behaviour while holding on to traditional family values. They will discuss decisions and explain them to their children. They will help the children to make up their own minds if possible. When necessary they will decide for them, but the decision is always negotiable.

Activity 4.2 Which of these four types of parent/child relationship would be the majority in your culture? Among your friends? Within your family? Which type would you personally favour? Using Hofstede's four dimensions where would you place each type of family on a 10-point scale?[2]

Parents and teachers

The type of relationship parents and children traditionally share will naturally be considered normal within the society into which one is born. It will naturally be present in educational relationships: teachers are expected to be in complete control of what takes place within their classrooms, if the majority of parents belong to the first and third types described in the previous section. If parents are keen on developing the autonomy of their children (types four and two), they will be in favour of a co-operative type of methodology. The teacher is then expected to drop the authoritative style of teaching, and negotiate and communicate with his/her charges. Both styles of teaching occur in the Netherlands, sometimes within one school. A gradual shift seems to be taking place towards a more co-operative methodology, even in so-called denominational schools.

Activity 4.3 Which style of teaching is the dominant one within your country/school? Is this true for all levels of education/subjects? Are there any signs of impending changes?[3]

Clearly, changes in educational thinking will have a tremendous impact on the way a society deals with social relationships. If teachers are agreed on implementing a 'traditional' methodology, a society will almost certainly score high on 'power distance', perhaps also on 'collectivism', probably high on 'assertiveness' and perhaps on 'uncertainty avoidance' as well. If, however, the educational system is keen on developing 'autonomous behaviour', it seems likely that the scores on these four dimensions will be much lower.

It is interesting to speculate on which type of society will be happier: the one that insists on developing individual responsibility and power sharing, or the society that imposes traditional values (cf. Chapter 2, *Language and social intercourse*, activity 2.18 and the information provided in note 9).

Why develop learner autonomy

The answer is another question: Who else is to do the learning for the learner? Research has made it abundantly clear that 'learning is not a straightforwardly cumulative process, not simply a matter of the learner gradually adding more and more pieces to his stock of knowledge in the way that a child may add blocks of Lego to a developing shape. Rather, learning is to be seen as a process where each increment must be accommodated to what the learner already knows by various processes of adjustment and revision. New knowledge, in other words, necessitates the reorganization of existing knowledge.' (Little 1991 p15)

We organize our knowledge into schemata, mental templates for situations, which allow us to react more or less 'automatically' in a setting that looks like one we know and afterwards compare it with the schema. 'We are always trying out new sensory information against our resident schemata, seeing what mold they fit among the multitudes in our cephalic library. And the human brain seems to have acquired an almost unlimited capacity to create new schemata. Indeed, given our compulsions to distinguish this from that and thus create dichotomies, we might be said to have a passion for new schemata, creating a new mold when the old ones don't quite fit.' (Calvin 1986 p191) Learning viewed as the creation of new schemata is obviously an individual process, although it is possible through the intermediary of language to share what one has learned with other human beings.

Human communication makes extensive use of schemata. We interpret a string of sounds by comparing it with an auditory schema in the brain, coming up with a set of associations from memory, and recognize words. Similarly, we interpret strings of words using mental rules for word order, so that 'John called Frances' carries a different message from 'Frances called John'. But not all languages use the same basic order of sentence-parts. Japanese uses the order subject - object - verb, and classical Arabic has verb - subject - object, which creates difficulties for people who are used to subject - verb - object.

Syntax plays its part in communication. At least as important is correct use of interactional rules, ie application of rules concerning 'who opens a conversation', 'who is allowed to interrupt the speaker', 'how one places an interruption', 'what facial expression one uses to show interest' and all these other verbal and non-verbal signals that show that the speaker and the listener are aware of how to carry on a conversation politely and properly. In short, the study of 'discourse' is at least as important as the study of grammar and syntax when one is learning another language.

Learning to cope in another culture creates difficulties. Different individuals belonging to the same culture will often use individual schemata more or less different from those used by others. The explanation lies partly with the individual's social background and education, partly with the sub-culture(s) the individual identifies with. The learner, in meeting the new language and culture, has to create new schemata to cope with other rules of behaviour, both verbal and non-verbal. In due course, perhaps not immediately (cf. Chapter 1, *Learning a new code*, and Kellerman 1987), learners discover that using the rules and schemata that apply in their native culture creates communication difficulties. This will prepare them for the next stage of mastery. But this requires a willingness on the part of the learner to become part of the other culture. Fortunately, all human beings know instinctively how to go about dealing with the problem. Before the age of puberty they manage quite efficiently on the whole, but even after the 'critical period' the language instinct may still function very well.

The critical period is generally assumed to be the age before which exposure to (another) language must have taken place to prepare the learner for (alternative ways of) communicating with human beings. I suspect, but have not found relevant research yet, that much of the difficulty lies with the traditional learning activities still favoured in many schools. If language teachers insist on the approach recognized within their cultural framework as the most efficient, the chances are that at least some pupils will show signs of *anomie* (cf. Chapter 1, *Cultural achievement*). The danger of *anomie* can be avoided through suitable stimulating and motivating activities, particularly those that allow the learner to control his/her individual learning process (see the next chapter). It is necessary always to be aware of this potential problem, particularly in a social environment that insists on immigrants conforming to the dominant culture, allowing no room for a pluralist perspective.

Activity 4.4 What is the official attitude towards the integration of migrants (first and second generation) into your country? Do all comers have to learn the majority language? What level of mastery is required? Does the policy work?[4]

Responsible citizenship

The refusal to face the consequences of the multicultural society learners (and indeed all citizens) need to come to terms with will often lead to explosions of ultra-nationalism and violence towards other cultures and social groups. Such situations will, and do, occur in many countries. Young men in particular will be attracted by alternative approaches to organizing their lifestyle, when they feel the need to 'prove themselves', 'to be appreciated and respected as a person'. The urge to join one or other sub-cultural movement will be especially strong, when the home culture allows little freedom of movement, or initiative, in short: insists on conformity. Such sub-cultures are a particular, but not exclusive, feature of cultures where power distance is great and where joining one or other sub-culture is virtually the only way of making known one's disapproval of the way society is organized. But there are of course other areas of social interaction that may offer opportunities for protest.

Becoming a responsible member of a country's population involves receiving and accepting responsibility, and if one does not learn this at home, the best alternative is probably school.

Activity 4.5 The other day while travelling on the local bus I overheard a conversation between a local boy and girl. He was telling her about being caught by the police for speeding in a built-up area. (The speed limit is 50 kms, and he was doing 100 kilometres per hour.) The affair cost him Dfl. 500, which is a lot of money for an eighteen-year-old, and he was obviously very angry. The girl reacted by asking if he would in future comply with the speed limit. His reaction was: 'Of course not! But I will have to drive a bit slower, say 70–75 kilometres per hour, or it's going to cost me too much money.'

If this were one of your pupils, how would you deal with the situation? Probably not on the bus, but in one of your classes?[5]

So often people are required/expected to obey rules without any form of explanation as to why the rule exists in the first place. Traffic regulations are one example; school rules another. An accepting and open atmosphere in the school, in which learners and teachers can discuss matters, helps towards educating the learner to responsible citizenship. The foreign language class could then develop into a non-threatening environment in which to develop a taste for alternatives to one's own cultural value system.

The next problem needing attention is then the question of the teacher's contribution to the language learning process. Before we go into activities that will contribute to developing the learner's communicative competence, we need a workable definition of the concept.

The definition of communicative competence

The ability to use a language that is not one's own, skilfully and effectively, requires a great deal more than just knowing vocabulary and grammar. It also involves inside knowledge of the foreign culture in the sense of: what topics are better avoided, what topics are safe, how to repair misunderstandings and social clumsiness, and a host of other problems which all come under the heading of communicative competence. The concept was launched by Hymes (1972) in his reaction to Chomsky's use of linguistic competence as: '... the competence underlying actual language use, the ability and knowledge to understand and speak a language' (Van Essen 1989a p4). It may be defined as 'the ability to use language appropriately and efficiently, making use of linguistic, pragmatic, discoursal, strategic and social competence on the basis of sociocultural and metacommunicative awareness ... Using language appropriately and efficiently requires an audience and a purpose, ie language is used to convey and negotiate meanings or social knowledge.' (Willems 1993b p24)

The various competencies learners have acquired in their respective native languages need to be translated into English. The learner needs to realize as well that there may not be a direct correspondence between the schemata he/she applies in the mother tongue and those in the foreign language. When the learner is given the central position in the learning process, it is also important to realize that the acquisition of overall communicative competence is a gradual process and takes time.

For practical purposes I will follow the explanation of the relationships between these competencies as set out in *Attainment Targets for Foreign Language Teacher Education in Europe* (Willems 1993b). In the context of the relationships between the competencies stated below, a distinction is made between declarative and procedural knowledge. Declarative knowledge refers to analytic skills, the ability to formulate 'rules' of language behaviour. Linguistic, pragmatic and discourse competence come under this label. Procedural knowledge is to do with the application of such rules, the skill of using them appropriately, even skilfully, as required by the context of communication. It is to do with planning our negotiation and thus comes under strategic competence.

Overall communicative competence may be subdivided as follows:

- *linguistic competence* refers to the speaker/listener's 'receptive and productive command of the grammar, the articulation, the idiom and vocabulary of the target language in oral and written form.' (Ibid. p25)
- *pragmatic competence* is the speaker/listener's 'receptive and productive command of direct and indirect, both conventional and unconventional speech act realisations in all situations not involving specific slang or restrictive code utterances. The command of paralinguistic skills involving verbal and nonverbal strategies (irony, gesture, etc) is an integral part of this competence.' (Ibid.)
- *discourse competence* consists of the 'repertoire of linguistic devices (and the skill in using them) to make discourse coherent. This involves such things as initiating interaction or opening a text, intervening as a listener, applying time-gaining and turn-taking "gambits" and concluding an exchange.' (Ibid.)
- *strategic competence* refers to the

> ability to process language data efficiently and appropriately under the constraints that characterise natural interaction, such as time constraints and limited short term memory. In other words, this competence refers to the skill to make the best use of the available linguistic, pragmatic and discourse knowledge. Speech acts and discourse formulas cannot be used randomly. Strategic competence enables us to link up our linguistic and pragmatic competence to the context or situation we find ourselves in, in order to reach the intended communicative purpose satisfactorily. Strategic competence is based on our specific mental make-up: our cultural identity. In foreign language communication, which is of necessity cross-cultural, our strategic competence needs to be cross-cultural as well, ie we need to learn to use another 'procedural knowledge' than we use in our mother-tongue. We need to master another strategic competence based on our socio-cultural knowledge of the target language community. Naturally we shall need to compensate for insufficient mastery at times. Skills needed for this come under 'strategic competence' as well.
> (Ibid.)
>
> Social knowledge differs from (sub-)culture to (sub-)culture. Therefore awareness of one's own and one's interlocutor's *socio-cultural knowledge* is required to make cross-cultural negotiation of meaning effective and efficient. It is also desirable for easy communication that the interactants have developed an adequate *meta-communicative awareness*, ie that they know about and can recognise strategies and procedures employed in communication.
> (Ibid. pp25–6)

Figure 1 illustrates the relationships between the components of communicative competence.

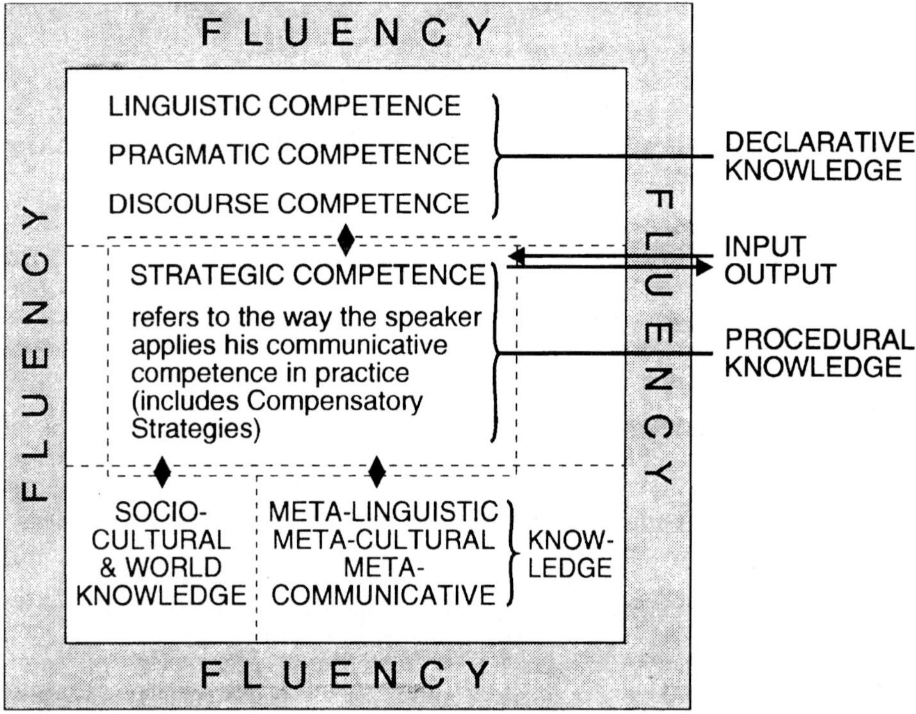

Figure 1 Components of communicative competence (Willems 1993b p26)

The model described here has a number of advantages. It allows for individual differences in (foreign) language command and it may be the starting point of the description of different levels in the acquisition process. Put differently: it can be used as the starting point for the identification of an individual's level of achievement at a given moment in the learning process and similarly as the basis for the description of different levels of language command. The model makes useful distinctions between 'the knowledge the learner brings into the classroom', 'what it is he needs to learn' and finally 'what areas of declarative knowledge are available on which to draw for developing the learner's competence'. In the final chapter of this book the implications this model has for language teaching materials and for the language teacher's approach to classroom activities will be considered more fully.

The problem of motivation

One aspect of learning not covered in the model discussed in the last section is 'motivation': the willingness on the part of the learner to accept voluntarily a task which may not always be very exciting but which he/she recognizes as useful towards achieving the objective. Teachers in many countries often complain about lack of motivation in their learners. Apparently their underlying assumption runs something like this: 'It is a privilege to be allowed to attend classes in my school, therefore learners are motivated to work hard to master what I have to offer.' However, when they compare the learners' interest in digging into their subject with the enthusiasm learners bring to out-of-school activities, there is a mismatch. All teachers know that when a learner is highly motivated the learning process makes great strides. Unfortunately, some of them are apparently disinclined to find out from the learners what type of activities help them come to grips with the subject.

The attitude occurs in many schools as the following shows. It is part of the Dutch ethos to be aware of the need to be able to communicate in other languages. Selling a language is no problem. TV language courses enjoy tremendous popularity to judge from the amount of interest in *Por Favor* (Spanish) or *Ni Hai!* (Modern Chinese), when they were offered, and many others. This does not mean that languages enjoy equal status and popularity. Languages taught in the educational system are not as popular as they ought to be. A language will become a subject of the school curriculum if its economic importance to the state can be proven. For the Dutch, this is obviously true of English, German, French, Spanish and to a lesser extent Russian. However, the numbers of pupils in upper secondary education taking these languages are totally unrelated to economic figures. Dutch exports to English-speaking countries are about 20 per cent of the total export figure, whereas virtually every secondary school pupil takes English in the school-leaving exam. The export figures for Germany are about 60 per cent, but less than 15 per cent of the school population takes this language in their final exam. One explanation may be that these 15 per cent recognize that they need German, and English, for their career; their motivation is mainly *instrumental* (extrinsic). *Integrative* (intrinsic) motivation in foreign language learning becomes apparent in the wish to learn languages outside the formal school setting.

Activity 4.6 The Dutch have a saying: 'I buy in my language and I sell in yours', reflecting the economic value of knowing languages. Does your language have similar expressions? Is economic relevance rather than inherent worth brought forward as an argument for the inclusion of foreign languages into the school curriculum in your country?[6]

Learning a foreign language: motivation

There are obviously factors which contribute to the motivation of learners, as there are factors which demotivate. Some of these are part of the classroom: they have to do with the relationship between teacher and class, while others belong to the myths of education: they are part of the cultural environment to which we belong. I shall begin with the latter.

Some cultures qualify language learning as an activity a man should not really be interested in. He should give his attention to those subjects on the school curriculum that he needs for a career: subjects like maths and economics, which really exercise the brain.

There are a number of approaches to overcoming this problem. Sometimes it may be enough to indicate that most of the relevant literature for a particular subject is published in the foreign language – for example on management problems, where German publications are a rich source of useful information and suggested solutions. The role of English in this context is mostly obvious. So obvious in fact, that in one of the upper forms of a primary school in Portugal – a country that scores high on the masculinity index – it was the boys who asked the English-speaking visitor all the questions, whereas the girls said very little even after repeated prompting (personal experience).

Learning another language does not just consist of learning lists of grammatical structures and pages of vocabulary. In fact, all learners know instinctively that they will use this language for communication and that learning to use this new, constantly changing medium means having to come to terms with different ways of viewing the world. In other words learning activities must be relevant to the learners' instinctive notion of what language learning is all about. Activities in the language class need to be relevant. In Chapter 5 I will go into the selection of learning activities. Here I wish to point out that for all learners the great motivating impetus is the discovery that the teacher gives them responsibility for carrying out the things they can do responsibly. This means that, as teachers, we have to be aware of what this might mean in terms of the cultural backgrounds of our learners.

Activity 4.7

In some cultures teachers are traditionally invested with great status. They are the people who decide what is taught and how to deal with teaching the subject. Learners are expected to be docile, listen, and learn what the teacher tells them to learn. If a learner with this type of background were to join one of your classes, how would you help him/her understand about the status of teachers in your culture?[7]

Teaching English in the multicultural classroom

There are three parties involved in setting up the multicultural classroom. First of all there is the government and its representatives. If a government subscribes to the notion that respect for and understanding of other cultures is necessary, and decides, as a consequence, to create conditions which will help to achieve this objective in education, there are some measures that might be introduced. For example, adequate provision for the training and, if necessary, retraining of teachers makes it a lot easier to achieve the aim. Special working groups might be set up to examine existing EFL (and other subjects) materials with regard to attitudes towards other cultures. And many more suggestions may be possible, all to do with creating conditions which give all the learners an equal chance to achieve the educational goals that best suit their personality (cf. Rey 1986 Chapter 5).

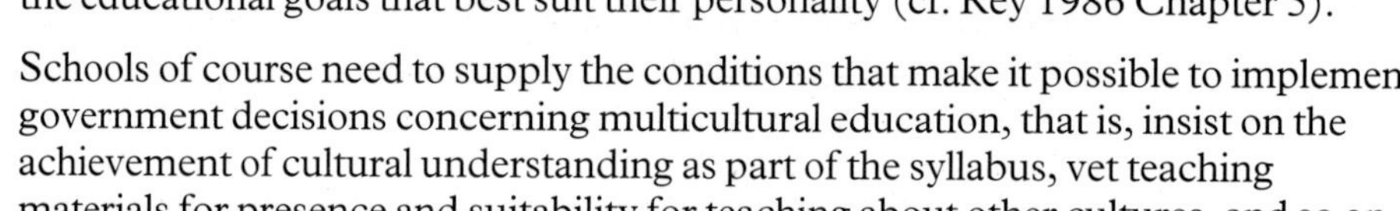

Schools of course need to supply the conditions that make it possible to implement government decisions concerning multicultural education, that is, insist on the achievement of cultural understanding as part of the syllabus, vet teaching materials for presence and suitability for teaching about other cultures, and so on.

Activity 4.8 Examine your present textbook for learning English, or another foreign language, for its attitude to other cultures, in particular the way other cultures (not just British or American) are represented.[8]

The teacher's contribution

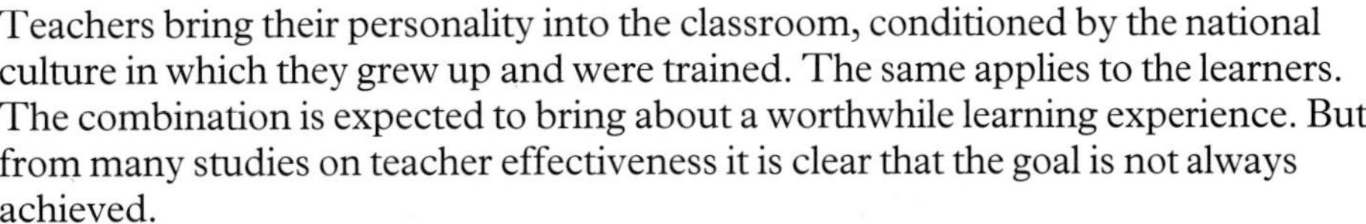

Teachers bring their personality into the classroom, conditioned by the national culture in which they grew up and were trained. The same applies to the learners. The combination is expected to bring about a worthwhile learning experience. But from many studies on teacher effectiveness it is clear that the goal is not always achieved.

Language classes do not enjoy great popularity in many countries. Part of the explanation lies in the way teachers see their task as purveyors of linguistic information. Their pupils may be especially interested in using the foreign language for communication, but what they get is a diet of linguistic facts. A second cause may be the totally inadequate way in which teachers are trained for the work they are expected to do – a feature they share with most of western Europe, apparently. Edelhoff (1989) in his report to the Council of Europe put it like this:

> **There was general agreement that many teachers feel anxious and threatened by the demands made on them by the move to a communicative approach to language teaching. These anxieties derive in part from:**
> **– a feeling of inadequate language competence in a communicative sense. This is more marked among primary teachers who are not narrowly specialised teachers of language only.**
> **– New knowledge in areas which teachers themselves did not study during initial or ongoing professional development – areas such as pragmatics, sociolinguistics, etc.**
> **– The need to accept educational views and values which are felt to be contrary to cherished traditions or to which the teacher does not subscribe. In particular, the change of teacher-role to that of facilitator of pupil-centred learning poses problems for teachers in a culture or school environment which works predominantly on an authoritarian, 'top-down' model.**
> **(Council of Europe 1989 p73)**

Edelhoff's report was concerned with teachers' difficulties in the initial years, phase one of learning a foreign language in state-supervised education. Phase two, in both general education and vocational education, is the concern of a new Council of Europe Project which started after Project 12 was finalized in Strasbourg in 1988. Participants in this conference were well aware of prospective problems awaiting teachers of foreign languages in the near future. The final report of Project 12 contained ten pages of recommendations relevant to this area of language education (Council of Europe 1989, pp77 ff.).

One of the problems recognized by the participants of the conference in Strasbourg in 1988 is the traditional approach to language teaching in the upper levels of secondary education: the cultural link with literature most language teachers insist on. Dealing with literature, the literary canon, along well-known traditional lines is not very motivating, even for learners who have developed an interest in reading books. The top-down approach, mentioned above, is mostly counter-productive and should be changed into a more learner-centred methodology.

The way in which this can be best achieved has been discovered by many individual teachers, and analysed and described by countless researchers. The result of all this activity can be found in many publications (eg in Holec 1988; Little 1991; or: Legutke and Thomas 1991). All insist on a shift of focus from the teacher as instructor to manager of the learning process, thus making the learners responsible for their progress towards mastery of the foreign language.

In many traditional classrooms involving the learners and giving them responsibility for their own progress is very hard to achieve simply because the school culture will insist on observing a firm degree of power distance. Teachers are expected to lecture their class on how to achieve the objectives of the course and set their pupils to work. As soon as the noise level goes beyond a certain limit, as often happens with oral activities, a senior teacher will storm into the classroom and call the class to order. The pressure to concentrate mainly on silent activities is very strong. Language teaching textbooks in such cultural surroundings usually conform to this traditional view of the language class. The problem for many progressive language teachers is therefore twofold: they have to adopt a new approach to their subject and they have to come to terms with colleagues and the management of the school concerning their innovative approach.

The development of learner autonomy is, nevertheless, a condition for developing mutual cultural respect and understanding, both within the classroom context and among nationalities. For one thing, language comes under instinctual rather than learnt behaviour. The language faculty is part of human nature. It develops autonomously, given an environment that allows the child to develop its communicative abilities (cf. Pinker 1994 and Jackendoff 1993 for a recent discussion).

This is the situation for learning the native language (L1): is it relevant to learning a second language (L2)? Much research is available on learning another language, particularly outside the classroom. The main conclusion must be that there is a parallel between learning the first and the second language, although there are a large number of variables that we cannot control (cf. Larsen-Freeman and Long 1991). For the L2 classroom setting and its relationship to L2 learning the problem is that to a large extent L2 teaching still suffers from the past in many respects. One way out of the problem may well be simply to accept that teachers do not and cannot control what their learners learn. Therefore helping learners to learn may give them a chance to discover that individuals are different from each other and need to be respected for that reason, as well as that the same applies to respecting other cultures.

Activity 4.9 What was the view of your English teacher (in secondary school) concerning learner autonomy? Did he/she ever express a point of view? How did it show in class management?[9]

The place of the learner

The third partner in the process of achieving multicultural understanding is the learner. Learners come into schools with important differences in individual cultural outlook. Obviously they also share a great deal, but most of their notions concerning the relationships between people are based on what they have picked up at home. A broad generalization may be that pupils from an upper and middle class background will not be too much impressed by notions of power distance, or individuality, or male superiority, or even uncertainty avoidance. Their background will have taught them that they already have social status. It will not have made them too receptive to uncritical acceptance of a teacher's authority. On the other hand they would probably be open to being given responsibility for their learning progress. Pupils from a working class and perhaps also those of a lower middle class background will probably (have to) observe the cultural rules of their country much more closely than children from a higher social level. They may well be open to bearing responsibility, but will need careful guidance as to what this means and what is involved in being responsible for one's own learning. Placing this mixture into one classroom with pupils from immigrant parents might well develop into a very explosive mixture, if the class teacher is an authoritarian, and not aware of his/her own, and their, cultural convictions and hang-ups.

Cultural understanding

It has been shown many times that mutual understanding between different cultures can be achieved, if one allows children to find out about each other (cf. Byram *et al.* 1994). The division between Catholic and Protestant areas in Belfast is very strictly observed (perhaps relations will improve over time, when the governments of Britain and Ireland have come to an agreement that all the parties involved find acceptable), but when children from both sides were brought together in a non-threatening environment friendly relations were established within a very short time. Maintaining the friendly relations after returning to their home ground turned out not to be so simple, of course.

Cultural understanding of cultures other than one's own can really only come about through understanding one's own culture. Alix and Kodron (1988) report an interesting venture in cross-cultural communication. They invited their pupils to make a silent video recording of 'an ordinary day at school' for their fellow pupils in France and Germany respectively. This was the start of a very interesting learning experience which ended in a most rewarding mutual visit. Similar activities involving pupils in coming to mutual understanding will be discussed in Chapter 5.

The main conclusion to be drawn from learning experiments in internationalization is that such activities can only be successful when learners are involved in every stage of the planning of the project and have responsibility for its execution. One important proviso must be made, ie that teachers give their learners sufficient latitude towards responsibility. Edelhoff (1984) reports in 'The Lancaster Outing' how cross-cultural teaching is most effective when teachers have been through the experience first. In other words: the best cross-cultural teacher is he/she who has personally experienced a culture shock.

Negotiating agreement on objectives and learning activities

In many countries teachers are arriving at a crossroads. They have to make up their minds whether to continue teaching in a traditional authoritarian way or to become managers of the learning processes of their pupils. 'For too long teaching has, probably unwittingly, worked towards keeping the learner dependent on the teacher, and by being error-centred, towards causing the learner to lose self-respect instead of gaining it.' (Willems 1993b p27)

Switching the focus away from error to successfully negotiating a communicative activity can only be realized by allowing the learner to try out what he/she has mastered so far. Learners, when asked to carry out a communication task, will make mistakes, but recognition of one's shortcomings helps towards overcoming them. Elaine Tarone shows that the occurrence of linguistic errors in the learner's use of the second language varies from one situation to another. This variation, to a large extent, depends on factors like interlocutor, ie who the subject is speaking to and what his/her status is; topic, what the status of the topic of the conversation is in terms of formality of the language required; and social norms, ie awareness on the part of the second language user of the necessity to adapt his/her use of the foreign language to the setting in which it is used (Tarone 1988 Chapter 3, and the discussion on objectives in the previous chapter).

The emphasis on avoiding errors is also to some extent a left-over from the days of audio-lingual drilling, when teachers tried to stamp out errors, as these represented a lack of 'automation' in the learner's handling of language patterns (cf. Brown 1987, pp62 ff.). These days we are aware that learning a skill, any skill, be it driving a car, swimming, writing, even speaking a foreign language, is to a large extent a process of trial and error. Of course my driving instructor did not take me out into dense rush-hour traffic in my first lesson. Rather he carefully guided me through a number of 'graded' situations, so that in due course he felt I could be trusted to cope with most everyday traffic settings. Of course I made mistakes after passing my driving test, but they were never fatal, and I gradually became better able to avoid accident-prone situations.

Learners need their teacher's trust and co-operation in the language learning process. There are activities and ways of organizing these which stimulate the learner's use of the foreign language (more of this in the next chapter). In the rest of this chapter I will discuss ways of selling the idea to the learners.

Much of what follows is based upon personal experience and the observation of classrooms in action in various countries in Europe. There is a striking difference in teachers' attitudes to learners in much of northern Europe and most of the middle and south. Teachers in southern Europe, as well as large parts of Germany, France, Britain and the Netherlands, on the whole act as if they are firm adherents of a tradition of large power distance. The effect of this for the communicative classroom has been described in an interview by Professor G.J. Westhoff as 'teaching learners about driving a car by the teacher taking the driving seat and explaining it all to his thirty-odd passengers who are only expected to watch.'

There are, as always, many individual teachers in all of these countries who are less concerned with their status and interact on a footing of equality with their learners and students (cf. Holec 1988). Scandinavian teachers are apparently much less concerned with power distance, and one gets the impression there that negotiation between teacher and pupil is normal, and works very well.

Why negotiate?

Negotiating a switch from the teacher-dominated to the learner-centred classroom can only be achieved if all the parties involved are in agreement. 'Negotiation is a discussion between two or more parties with the apparent aim of resolving a divergence of interest and thus escaping social conflict' (Pruitt and Carnevale 1993 p2). This definition is useful, because it offers an opportunity to clear up a few misunderstandings in the relationships between teachers and their classes and among the pupils within each form. When the teacher only operates from a position of power, allows no discussion, will not accept learners' contributions to the learning process, there is no negotiation taking place. And, of course, learners will pursue their own interests and perhaps negotiate their attitude towards the teacher among themselves.

Activity 4.10 The management of the school wishes to catch up on present-day tendencies towards learner autonomy and independence. In order to bring about a change in 'school culture' they suggest that subject departments should think about the consequences of more involvement of learners in decisions concerning textbooks and teaching/learning materials, appointments of staff, study courses (content, grading, testing, etc), timetabling of subjects, and other relevant areas. You are asked to draw up a discussion paper for the department setting out what changes in teacher attitude towards the learners need to be effected and what types of training might be helpful to bring about the attitudinal changes the school management has in mind.[10]

Particularly in a multicultural group the often-heard assumption that the class is the enemy, with all its possible negative connotations, is generally not true, except when the learners are forced to unite against patently hostile treatment. In fact, however, cases of violence against teachers have been reported in the press, where individual learners or groups of them threatened, sometimes even took, physical action against a teacher. Special counselling telephone numbers are available in some cities in the Netherlands, to help individual teachers deal with a situation that has patently got out of hand.

It is unwise to treat the group of learners the teacher is negotiating with as one group sharing a common interest in their relations with the teacher. One solution that generally works is to accept that learners can be responsible for their own behaviour. This responsibility must at the same time include learners accepting that others may have different opinions from their own on a variety of topics and that this must be accepted and tolerated. This change of attitude cannot be forced upon a group of learners but must be negotiated. The aim of the negotiation is, in a sense, to achieve an agreement between the individual learner and the teacher about the aims of the course in English they are attending and the way its goals will be reached. The goals include acceptance of other cultural behaviour, naturally.

Breen (1985) describes eight features of the language classroom which are always to a greater or lesser extent present.

> **The classroom culture is:**
> **(1) *interactive*;**
> **(2) *differentiated* (ie although the classroom appears as one social unit it is always a composition of many social realities with often conflicting views of the world, of language and of learning);**
> **(3) *collective* (ie it constitutes itself in the constant interplay between individual and collective processes);**
> **(4) *highly normative* (ie any formal and institutionalized L2 learning situation cannot escape the fact that it is evaluative in nature, engaging teacher and taught in continually judging each other in various respects and on various levels);**

(5) *asymmetrical* (ie asymmetrical relationships with respective roles and role expectations do not only exist between groups and sub-groupings; in institutionalized settings there is a clear connection between asymmetry and power relations, which have a decisive impact on the learning process);
(6) *inherently conservative* (ie as with any group, language classes have a tendency to establish their own rules, develop their own rituals and styles, which may become quite resistant to innovation and change);
(7) *immediately significant* (ie the learning experience itself takes place in the here and now);
(8) *jointly constructed*: What someone learns in a language class will be a dynamic synthesis of individual and collective experience. Individual definitions of the new language, of what is to be attended to as worth learning, of how to learn, and personal definitions of progress will all interact with the particular classroom culture's definitions of each of these things ... The language I learn in a classroom is a communal product derived through a jointly constructed process.
(Breen 1985 pp148–9, quoted in Legutke and Thomas 1991 p14)

Strategies for negotiation

Having decided to negotiate the learning process with the class, it helps to decide on a strategy, 'a plan of action, specifying broad objectives and the general approach that should be taken to achieve them.' (Pruitt and Carnevale p3). Pruitt and Carnevale distinguish five basic strategies that are used in negotiation. Two of these apply when unworkable situations have arisen, when the possibilities of all other strategies have been exhausted: 'inaction' and 'withdrawal'. The terms are self-explanatory, and since they only apply when a deadlock has been reached, I will not discuss them further. The remaining three may all come in handy at particular moments in the classroom context.

The first is *concession making*. From the label the function of the strategy is clear: it consists of lowering one's aims, reducing one's demands, hoping thus to save at least something from what one originally had in mind. When each party has made its position clear, this strategy is useful to get the negotiations underway. At the same time it may be helpful to remember that in many cultures making a concession may be read as a sign of weakness.

The second strategy is *contending*. It is the opposite of concession making, as its intention is to get the other party to make concessions. It is the strategy one adopts when starting from a position of power. The stronger party in the negotiation may threaten to use force when the other does not change his position, or clearly indicate that there is no chance of a concession on a particular issue.

Opting for either the first or the second of these strategies has a lot to do with the culture within which one teaches and/or with the personality of the teacher. This is something the teacher should be aware of.

Activity 4.11 Think of one or two occasions when you used a concession-making or a contending strategy in your dealings with a group of learners. Did it work? Or would it have been better for the relationship between you and the group of learners to discuss the issue in more depth and try to find an acceptable solution?[11]

Problem solving is the final, and to my mind generally the most constructive, strategy in dealing with groups of learners. It implies that each party knows and appreciates the other's position, and wishes to work towards a solution to the problem that is the best for everyone involved. The tactic adopted by all the parties is called *joint decision making*. In the educational literature the outcome of this type of negotiation is often called 'a learning-teaching contract', which states what the contribution of each party will be and the expected outcome of the process.

The contribution of the learner will be motivated activity to benefit from what is offered during the course. The teacher's contribution consists of selecting relevant learning situations and activities that allow for individual differences in needs, learning styles, and preferences.

Planning an activity

Once the role of the learner as a responsible participant in the learning process has been accepted, and the teacher allows the learner to contribute responsibly to the negotiation of aims, goals and learning activities to be adopted in the multicultural language class, the following model, in three stages, may help towards agreeing on a learning contract between teacher and learner.

The first stage involves planning and exploration. The activity is offered and can be discussed in terms of: do we understand what it involves; have we got the necessary linguistic tools available; what are the criteria for successful completion of the task; etc. A simple way to deal with this stage is to ask the group of learners to note down their individual answers to these questions. Then discuss and compare these in small groups in order to come up with, perhaps, a few areas of expected difficulty the teacher may be able to resolve beforehand.

Once the group is happy with the task it has been set, the signal is given for them to do the activity. The role of the teacher then is to observe, give help 'if and when required', and keep an eye on the clock.

The third and last stage consists of evaluation. The basic question is: 'Did it work?' The learners have to answer individually whether they found the activity useful in terms of the questions put to them in stage one: what sort of unexpected difficulties had to be overcome, and whether they managed to overcome them in English. What did they learn from carrying out the activity?

This simple plan may be adapted to the carrying out of any activity offered within the textbook or outside it. My personal experience is that learners quickly pick up the idea that learning is their individual responsibility and that they are expected to react critically to activities they are offered, which in its turn can be an eye-opener to all concerned.

Conclusion

A knowledge of languages, including knowledge about languages and a measure of cultural awareness, is necessary as a part of every citizen's educational background in his/her contacts with other cultures. Misunderstandings between cultures lead to bad feelings, animosity, stereotyping, discrimination and worse, and may be the cause of violence and war (cf. the situation in the former Yugoslavia in the early 1990s), and for that reason alone need to be avoided. To achieve optimal results from learning activities in the language class the learner must be in charge of the learning process. In this chapter I have tried to clear up a number of issues to do with developing learner autonomy.

Notes

1 One would expect that in Britain some time would be spent on the teaching of German and French. In other countries English and German might be taught, and perhaps French as an alternative in countries close to France. The curriculum would allow little time for oral skills development; most of the available time will be spent on the liberal arts and Culture (with a capital C), unless T-level type objectives have been introduced for foreign languages. (See Chapter 3, note 7.)

2 There may be a link with social status, the lower classes being more represented among types 1 and 3, and the middle classes in types 2 and 4, but the report did not discuss this point. On the scale of power distance type 3 would probably end close to the top followed by types 1, 2 and 4, which would in my view probably score around 4/5; the dimension assertivity vs modesty would probably show the same result; the dimension individual vs. collective (individual at the top) would give the order types 1, 2, 4, 3; the dimension of uncertainty avoidance might show type 3 near the top, followed by 4, 2, 1, where type 4 would score around 5. Hofstede would probably agree with me that most children would be very happy to grow up in a family that scores around 5 on each dimension.

3 It is an interesting question whether the recommendations made by the Council of Europe working group on modern languages on the development of learner autonomy would have been promoted so enthusiastically if the group had comprised more traditionally oriented members of the teaching profession than it did. The more influential members apparently came from institutions, such as CRAPEL in Nancy, France, where innovative approaches were used and experiments were carried out in which learners could bring forward their views.

4 Micheline Rey (1986) discusses a number of dangers (Chapter IV) that may arise. One is the special provision of 'lessons in languages and cultures of origin' on top of the regular school timetable. This will isolate the children with a migrant background. Her solution is to include such lessons in the normal timetable and allow an element of choice to all children whether they will attend these lessons or not, or alternatively to set time apart for comparison of discoveries made in the field of culture and linguistics, which will lead to mutual enrichment.

5 Traffic is one area of behaviour where one sometimes feels that rules have been thought up by an official, behind his desk, who really has no driving experience at all. Clearly, if one needs an outlet for outraged feelings, flouting traffic regulations may help a little towards cooling down. In the Dutch cultural setting I would probably at a suitable moment ask the class to discuss 'speed limits' and their function in regulating the traffic. I might ask them to include the option of doing away with them altogether and discuss the effects of such a measure. Perhaps we might end up with a letter to the police or local Council with suggestions for improving traffic regulations.

In your class you might ask representatives of different cultures how long they would obey a red traffic light in a setting where there is no traffic to be seen (late at night, for example), if it remains red for longer than a given period of time, say, 30 seconds.

6 The Dutch expression is typically culture bound, since the Netherlands have amassed their wealth through trade with the countries of Europe, importing and exporting goods from Asia and elsewhere. If import and export is the mainstay of your country's economy, one might expect to find similar expressions in your language.

In the context of this activity students will find it useful to compare the arguments brought forward in favour of the inclusion of different languages, not only English, in the syllabus for secondary education. In the Dutch context a move is being made towards study profiles which will qualify students for entry into specified areas of study. Surprisingly, knowledge of foreign languages hardly figures in the discussion.

7 Probably negotiation is the best approach. Find out from your new learner what teachers in his/her home country are like. Are the sexes segregated, for example? If so, you will have to explain that in your

culture it is quite common for women to teach groups of men. Ask them to explain the roles of men and women in their culture, etc. Ask them to accept that cultures may differ in the way they deal with masculine and feminine. Introduce your culture's way of dealing with achieving educational objectives, ask them for comment and criticism, in short, respect them, asking them to respect you.

8 Many FL textbooks do not go beyond the provision of factual information about the country whose language they teach, nor do they provide for experiential learning in this area (through assignments, etc). Hardly any space is set aside to provide cultural information with regard to Hofstede's four dimensions discussed in Chapter 2, except perhaps incidentally. Even the recognition that the country concerned is not only inhabited by pure white, middle class, respectable citizens (happily married, with two children, a dog, a family car, a nice house, etc), but is actually a multilevel, multicultural society speaking the language in a variety of accents and dialects, is rare.

9 It may be helpful to relate your teacher's view of education with Hofstede's dimensions in Chapter 2. This may clear up anything you could not understand in his/her conduct towards learners.

10 What is necessary here is analysis of teacher attitudes to learners in terms of Hofstede's four dimensions (power distance, collectivism, assertivity, uncertainty avoidance). Changes in attitude towards learners should go towards the central areas of the scales and may be brought about by consciousness-raising activities conducted mainly by outsiders. Insiders could also run such sessions, but the most important condition is that all the people involved accept their approach as valuable, which may be problematical for people whose 'reputation' is generally known.

11 Beginning teachers in particular often have problems recognizing what the relationship between them and their pupils should be. Mostly the ideal, recognized by both learners and teachers, is the teacher who manages the learning process in such a way that learner needs are recognized and given room for exploration. At the same time, this teacher is recognized as an authority by the learners in cases where decisive action is needed. In this setting learner and teacher feel happy and relaxed; there is a lot of stimulating learning activity going on, even when perhaps the exercise is rather dull.

Suggestions for further study

The most complete statement of the results of the Council of Europe's group of experts on languages is *Systems Development in Adult Language Learning*, Strasbourg 1973. In this publication the first draft of the threshold level is to be found. JA van Ek reworked this original proposal into *The Threshold Level*, Strasbourg 1975. This publication formed the basis of *The Threshold Level for Modern Language Learning in Schools*, Wolters-Noordhoff-Longman, Groningen 1976. Subsequently, a level below the threshold level was formulated in JA van Ek, LG Alexander and MA Fitzpatrick, *Waystage English*, Pergamon Press 1977. In 1990 the original *Threshold Level* was published in a revised form: JA van Ek and JLM Trim, *Threshold Level 1990*, Strasbourg, Council of Europe Press 1991.

Comparable descriptions are available for all the languages spoken in Europe. For the main languages these include: *Le niveau seuil*, *Kontaktschwelle Deutsch*, *Un nivel umbral*, *Livello Soglia*, *Et taerskelniveau for dansk*, etc.

The Council of Europe publishes many other relevant titles: Peter S Green (ed.), *Communicative Language Testing* 1987; *Objectives for Foreign Language Learning*, Vol. 1 Scope (JA van Ek 1986), Vol. 2 Levels (JA van Ek 1987); *Autonomy and Self-directed Learning: Present Fields of Application* (Holec 1988); *Self-assessment of Foreign Language Skills: A Survey of Research and Development Work*, (Council of Europe 1984); *Communication in the Modern Languages Classroom*, (Sheils 1988), to name but a few.

The Dutch publications about language teaching objectives for stage one of secondary education can be found in: *Advies over de voorlopige eindtermen basisvorming in het voortgezet onderwijs, 9: Moderne vreemde talen*, Den Haag 1989. The objectives for modern languages themselves were subsequently translated and published by SLO, Foundation for Curriculum Development, Enschede 1989. A slightly different version of the original statement of objectives may be found in: Commissie Herziening Eindtermen, *Advies kerndoelen voor de basisvorming in het basisonderwijs en voortgezet onderwijs*. Den Haag 1990. Similar publications of objectives may be obtained in many countries, of course. The National Curriculum Council in Britain published its Consultation Report on Modern Foreign Languages in 1991. In Germany the Bundesländer have formulated objectives for phase one of foreign language learning along similar lines. For phase two the Council of Europe is preparing overviews of developments in its member states. A first publication is available in G Stoks, *Curriculum Development for Modern Languages in Upper Secondary General, Technical and Vocational Education, 15/16 – 18/19*, Strasbourg 1993.

The ATEE working group on the education and training of language teachers published their *Attainment Targets for Foreign Language Teacher Education*, Gerard M Willems (ed.), in 1993, in ATEE Cahiers, No. 5, which can be obtained from the Association of Teacher Education in Europe, 60, rue de la Concorde, B 1050 Brussels.

Dean G Pruitt and Peter J Carnevale, *Negotiation in Social Conflict*, Open University Press 1993, analyses all the known aspects of negotiation in a variety of contexts in depth. As such it might be very helpful for those who have little experience with this aspect of everyday life.

Chapter 5 Methodology: suggestions for dealing with intercultural education

Many people choose to accept unified belief systems which provide answers to the major problems concerning life, and save themselves the bother of further inquiry. Their needs are met by mythology.
(Robert Shapiro, *Origins*, London 1986 p37)

Introduction

EFL materials are undergoing a great deal of change. For English in particular the realization that it is often the lingua franca in cross-cultural encounters has important consequences for the classroom (cf. Willems 1993b section 2.2.2). And in this classroom many learners are obviously second or third generation immigrants, with all sorts of consequences for relations among learners and with teachers. Textbook writers are under great pressure to conform to developments and discoveries in the field of language learning and teaching research. At the same time publishers have to sell their products in a highly competitive market to language teachers educated and trained in an environment where learning a foreign language meant getting access to the culture, the literature, and the fine arts of the society using the language.

Over the past 25 years or so many of the ideas discussed in previous chapters have found expression in learning activities. On the basis of this discussion there are a number of criteria that language learning materials to be used in the multicultural classroom should reflect:

- due attention must be given to developing 'linguistic, pragmatic and discourse competence', ie 'declarative knowledge'.
  In order to achieve this efficiently:
  – the relationship between grammar and meaning in communication should be emphatically present;
  – the study of vocabulary should allow for the development of the 'context of meaning'.
- the development of 'strategic competence' is the main objective of all classroom EFL activities. Learners concentrate on developing their communicative competence in English – including the development of compensatory strategies – on the basis of relevant input materials.
  Implications are:
  – texts should be 'authentic' in the senses of: reflecting actual native speaker usage and being relevant to the learner;
  – text materials should reflect the actual, multicultural composition of countries where English is used as the native language;
  – learning activities should be oriented towards authentic communication;
  – learning activities should allow for reflection on quality.
- 'socio-cultural and world knowledge' underlie and feed strategic competence.
  This leads to the condition that:
  – text materials should respect cultural differences, both in native speaker usage and in lingua franca settings;

– learning tasks should be interesting, varied, relevant and challenging to the learner;
– learning tasks should allow for different learning styles.

- 'metalinguistic, metacultural and metacommunicative knowledge' are essential to the continued growth of strategic competence.
  This development can only take place within the individual learner, hence:
  – the development of learner autonomy should be a central issue, both in the textbook materials and in the EFL classroom.

In this chapter I will discuss a selection of these requirements in the light of discoveries mentioned before. My focus will continue to be on EFL in the multicultural classroom.

Dealing with structure

In many traditional classrooms the teacher regularly grabs the opportunity offered by the textbook to explain the rules of English grammar. The relevance of this teacher activity to the learning of English shows whenever the learners happen to find themselves in a communication situation and actually have to use English. The structure of a language is learnt through use, and reflection and analysis after the event, if necessary.

Learners discover the relevance of a rule when they discover the need for it, like a young child discovering the rule for the formation of the plural, for example. Stephen Krashen claims that there is a strict order of acquiring a number of structural rules. While there is no complete agreement on the hypothesis, Evelyn Hatch has this to contribute: 'While there is a good deal of argument about the degree of systematicity in Interlanguage, many researchers and teachers believe that the move from the beginning stages of learning to later fluency follows a sequence that is not random.' (Hatch 1983) The way human beings organize linguistic schemata in the brain does not necessarily correspond with the linguist's account of this in his grammar (cf. Chomsky 1965 p25; Pinker 1994 Chapter 4; Jackendoff 1993 Chapter 6).

Wilga Rivers said it long ago: 'Teach the language and not about the language' (*Teaching Foreign Language Skills*, 1968 p39). All the same, it may help the learning process along, if at the right moment the learner's attention is drawn to a specific language phenomenon. The use of discovery procedures in the learning of grammatical structure, pragmatics and discourse has been tried in many classes and with great success (eg Rinvolucri 1984; Frank and Rinvolucri 1987; Penny Ur 1988; Ruth Wajnryb 1990). Nevertheless, many textbooks do not yet dare go beyond this type of exercise:

> Put the words in the right order. Write the whole sentence down:
> 1. Cardiff ... · isn't it · these days · busy · 's · very ?
> 2. We're ... · for you · a · looking · for · post office
> 3. ...

The pattern is familiar and derives from the audiolingual era. What has the learner achieved when he/she gets the word order right? Does he/she understand the sentence structure of English better? I suspect some can do it and others can't, and nobody learns very much – after all it is a test, not a learning activity.

One of the ways in which we organize meaning is, of course, through word order: syntax.

farmer call boy

In English, and also in many other languages, word order is an indication of what the speaker intends to convey, reflecting what native speakers might call a 'natural order'. In this example most of us will read the collocation as '*farmer*' initiates action, '*call*' is the action and '*boy*' is the object undergoing the action. The same would be true of similar collocations, like: '*soldier ride horse*' or '*cow eat grass*'. (The idea is from Widdowson 1991 Part Two.)

Activity 5.1 Find out from speakers of other languages – both L1 and L2 – if this rule also applies in the languages they know.[1]

It is quite possible to introduce nuances of meaning into the above collocations. '*Farmer*' may be '*a farmer*' or '*the farmer*', which makes it possible to distinguish between '*farmer*' as a new item in the communication or one the speaker has mentioned before and wishes to recall at this moment. '*Boy*' can be dealt with in a similar way with similar results. In fact the speaker may wish to be even more explicit and indicate that he is concerned with '*a group of farmers*', or even '*a group of boys*'. He may wish to indicate one specific representative of either group – one close by or one farther away, and many other things.

The speaker may wish to make clear that the action is taking place at the moment of speaking, or that the action happened some time ago, or even that there is a relationship between this past action and present time, or that the action will take place at some future moment, or perhaps that the aspect of 'time' is not relevant to the present communication. In English, all these require 'manipulation' of the word '*call*' through additions to the word form or the addition of one or more auxiliaries (or 'modals') to express one or other aspect the speaker intends.

Activity 5.2 Find out, for the other languages you checked with in the previous activity, how these differences are indicated in each language.[2]

Languages vary a good deal in the formal techniques they use to express meaning. Some favour a fairly fixed word order (syntax); others prefer prosodic means (intonation and tones); others again use elements that are added at the beginning or at the end of a root word: prefixes and suffixes. Most languages are undogmatic and use a combination of these three processes.

English seems to prefer the use of function words to achieve its communicative ends, a quality it shares with many so-called creoles: languages which developed out of an elementary signalling system used for a restricted purpose (a pidgin), for example to make trade possible between people who do not share any other language, like the way you yourself behave when buying something in the market place or ordering something to eat in a restaurant in a country where you don't speak the language.

Formal means like the three mentioned above are one facility we have available to achieve the expression of meaning, of course. Words (the lexicon) are another.

A look at words

We use words daily to share meanings with whoever we wish to communicate with. But we don't usually ask ourselves if our interlocutor really understands exactly what we mean, until we discover a misunderstanding has occurred. This cannot always be solved in a simple manner, but when we share a mutual interest a great deal can be achieved: cf. the following bit of dialogue between a German male (GM) and a Polish female (PW) overheard in a Warsaw restaurant:

PW: We eat pancakes in Poland.
GM: What?
PW: Pancakes.
GM: Ah, keks. Yes, I like. And we have er ... it's meal and milk and eggs and so on. You know meal?
PW: Yes.
GM: And you bake it. In German it's called Eierpfannkuchen.
PW: ...?
(John Strange, personal communication)

Clearly they were talking about something similar, but somewhere the communication went awry. Perhaps the German was not paying sufficient attention to the Polish woman's contribution. Or perhaps GM is assertive in his contribution and PW too modest. One thing is clear to the observer: *pancakes* and *Eierpfannkuchen* have something in common, which perhaps the two interlocutors still have to discover.

Another reason why misunderstandings occur is that perhaps a key word in the communication means something different to our interlocutor. In the conversation between the German and the Polish woman above the topic had changed slightly:

GM: A salad. You know, it's green, a vegetable.
PW: ...?

Understanding fails because the German uses *salad* as a translation for the German word *Salat* (lettuce), which may have rung a bell with his interlocutor, only the Polish related word, *salatki,* is a mixture of pickled vegetables, usually carrot, red cabbage and root celery (John Strange, personal communication).

Words have two levels of meaning: one that is shared by all its users, and an individual, or associative, meaning. The first is found in dictionaries, whereas the other consists of emotional overtones we may experience when this particular word occurs and which we associate with it because of our personal experience (cf. the emotional overtones the word *tempest* may have for a person who played a part in a production of Shakespeare's play of that name, and for someone whose ship was wrecked in a tempest). Whenever I come across the word *cabbage*, my stomach reacts in a slightly unpleasant manner and I see in front of me a plate of somewhat slimy, greenish, watery, only half hot 'goo', which I am supposed to eat. I know that cabbage can be cooked differently, so that it appears crisp and firm, and hot, on your plate. Nevertheless, the first association persists and, whenever I am served cabbage, I have to consciously replace this association by another. Many people recall a slightly penetrating, not really very pleasant smell, which tends to persist in the house after a meal in which cabbage has figured. None of these associations has very much to do with the dictionary meaning:

cabbage /kæbidzj/ n 1 [C] a type of large round vegetable with thick green leaves wrapped round its short stem – compare LETTUCE 2 [U] the leaves of this vegetable used (usu. cooked) as food 3 [C] BrE Infml an inactive person who takes no interest in anything
(*Longman Dictionary of Contemporary English* Third edition p140)

The dictionary meaning is the largest common denominator of a word's meaning shared by its users. If, like a computer, we stored words with a fixed address in our memories, there would be few problems in communicating with each other. There would be one other problem, though: there would be no room for the extension of word meaning necessary to accommodate new developments in the real world, nor for creativity, particularly in the field of literature.

Unfortunately this is not the way our brain works. We store words in our memories associated with incidents which are partly shared with others, partly strictly private. Sometimes we find ourselves in a group of people we like to share our memories with. This sets 'our' use of words apart from the way outsiders use these same words. If the differences are manageable, we continue to communicate with them, until 'we don't need them any more'.

Activity 5.3 Write down your personal associations with these words: *window, book, tree, child.* Now check your private meanings against the definitions in one or two dictionaries. Are there overlaps in meaning, or perhaps none at all? Can you explain the similarities and differences between your private meanings and the dictionary definitions? If possible, compare your findings with others.[3]

When learning another language the meanings, ie individual associations, of particular words are sometimes carried over and used in the same way as at home (remember the dialogues between the German man and the Polish woman). In Chapter 1 I suggested that the language of the community of which one is a member is the focus of reference. Learning the language of a new speech community means: coming to terms with the way in which this speech community organizes meanings. This can of course best come about through direct experience with native speakers. However, exposure to authentic spoken and written language is a useful substitute when the learner's attention is drawn to 'interesting' features of the discourse.

Differences between languages may show in the way one language has two words for a thing, whereas another uses only one, or the other way round. (See Activity 1.14, and note 14, in Chapter 1.) Another problem arises when a particular concept in our language has only a partial translation in another language, or even no translation at all.

Activity 5.4 Look up the following English words in a bilingual dictionary: *province, privacy, Justice of the Peace, cup final, moorlands.*

Can you account for the peculiar translations of some of them? Look up the translations in a monolingual dictionary of your own language and the original words in a monolingual English dictionary. Can you explain the differences between the two sets of definitions?[4]

Part of the job of learning another language is concerned with becoming familiar with the way society is organized in the other country. Meanings are closely bound up with institutions and rituals, which may function differently from the ones we are familiar with.

The best way to go about this in class is to see to it that words get a context in which they function. Short extracts of a prose text or of verse may serve to illustrate a meaning. Advertisements, both printed and spoken, are a very useful source. Vocabulary has to become, hopefully, part of the learner's active resources for communication. This can be achieved to some extent by occasionally organizing a word network: learners are asked, starting from a central word, to show relations and associations this word has with other words in the language. (Ellis and Sinclair 1989 p36, show an interesting example, starting off with *politics*.). Learning lists of words with their translations in the learner's native language is mainly counterproductive. Meaning is best acquired through using words in a meaningful context.

How to organize learner interaction

'You can't say: "I want to ask a question" in a meeting, because it's not polite.' When in your own language this phrase, or its native language translation, would be perfectly acceptable, why is it found impolite in Britain?

The British, they say, are very sensitive to invasions of their privacy. So, any attempt at entering a British person's 'private domain' has to be preceded by elaborate apologies for the intrusion. This sort of politeness is now a quite common feature of courses in business English; irritation will not lead to the desired ending of a business conference, so ...

Activity 5.5 Make a list of phrases you might use in your own language, when 'invading a person's private domain', ie in situations like:

- beginning a conversation with someone you know, *and* with someone you don't know;
- closing a conversation with someone you know, *and* with someone you don't know;
- interrupting a conversation to ask a question, or to make a contribution to the conversation.

Then find their English equivalents. How do cultural differences show in the phrases you have collected?[5]

Activity 5.6 To varying degrees people on the continent of Europe tend to shake hands more frequently than British people. Make a list of non-verbal ritual signals commonly used by people in your culture, things like shaking hands, exchanging kisses, smiling at each other, looking each other in the eye, etc. Now compare the use of these both in your own country and in a British context – 'soap serials' will offer rich cullings of these.[6]

Knowing lists based on these and similar differences between everyday occurrences is not sufficient for the language learner to avoid cultural pitfalls. What is necessary is training in recognition, observation, understanding and participation in situations requiring the use of phrases like these, as well as appropriate non-verbal behaviour.

Recognition can be practised through aural training, both audio and video, using suitable texts. Understanding may be helped along by watching TV serials, followed by discussion and comparison of one's findings with what others have discovered. The training in awareness-raising is then rounded off by taking part in an oral activity, roleplay or otherwise. If at all possible, direct experience of the other culture should be part of the course and the learning process.

Implications for materials

In the preceding three sections I have drawn attention to aspects of language and culture that do not usually figure very prominently in language teaching materials. If the need for a mind open to the otherness of representatives of other cultures is agreed, materials writers must pay more than lip service to cultural differences. This requires a fair knowledge, and direct experience, on the part of the writers of at least two cultures.

At present textbooks are generally organized into units of reasonable length, allowing the learners to keep in view the end product they will have to deliver in due course. Planned in time, a unit may usually take from five to ten lessons. Each unit starts off with one or more texts, reading and/or listening, followed by activities to check understanding, perhaps including awareness-raising activities (A). Then follow exercises to train various elements of language, among them grammatical structure and vocabulary (B). Next comes a range of exercises allowing application of what has been trained, in a controlled format (C), followed by 'free' application of language use in a discussion or roleplay activity (D). The paradigm is familiar from various publications and linked with names like Candlin, Edelhoff, Piepho, Neuner, and others (cf. eg Candlin 1981). For convenience's sake I will use this paradigm to discuss some of the requirements we would like to see met in our materials.

Text materials

Activity 5.7 Would you consider the following text acceptable as input text in a textbook for beginners learning English as a foreign language?

– Your ball is on the table! Take it off the table and put it away!
– Where shall I put it?
– Put it away! Put it in the box under the table!
– Okay! Here I have the ball and I put it in the box under the table.
– Thank you, John.

Give as many reasons as possible for your judgement.[7]

Textbook writers find themselves in an awkward position. They are introducing a language, its structures, vocabulary and cultural conventions, to an audience that is often perhaps totally unfamiliar with these things. If the solution adopted is found unacceptable by the textbook's users, the author's work was in vain. How to get round this?

In the early 1970s many learners of English were confronted with E Frank Candlin's *Present Day English for Foreign Students* (London, 1972), which contained this dialogue (p14):

JOHN: I am a man. You are a woman.
MARY: I am Mary Brown. You are John Brown.
JOHN: This is a book. That is a pen.
MARY: What is this?
(...)
JOHN: Am I a man, Mary?
MARY: Yes, John, you are a man, and I am a woman.

This was great fun, and good for a laugh, since everybody recognized the artificiality of this setting. This textbook is of course dated, but it illustrates every textbook writer's dilemma. Learners have to become familiar with everyday words and phrases, have to learn to use them in everyday settings and contexts, eg when talking about their own background. In due course, fortunately, with increased knowledge of English, the dialogue material becomes more 'natural'. What about the following dialogue, from the same textbook?

MR BROWN: Well, that was a good game. The best we've seen this winter.
DAVID: Yes. Better than last week. Easthampton have a good team, but the Bishopton players won because they're faster.
MR BROWN: Come on, David. The crowd's moving. We'll catch that bus. Then we can meet Mother in town for tea.
DAVID: Who are Bishopton playing next week?
MR BROWN: Cardiff City, I think.
DAVID: Do you think they'll win?
MR BROWN: I don't know. In Wales rugger is more important than soccer, but Cardiff have a good team this year.
DAVID: Which team will win the Cup?
MR BROWN: ...
(p190)

It looks attractive enough; a conversation between father and son about the match they've both been watching, and about some other aspects of football in general. Still, there is a ring of insincerity, of 'not really what native speakers do on this sort of occasion'. Suddenly it becomes clear: both speakers use complete sentences, grammatically perfect, not a word out of place! Not at all like what happens in spoken forms of the language (cf. eg Sinclair and Coulthard 1975; McCarthy 1991; Hatch 1992). Apart from this, there is all the information that Mr Brown supplies to his son, as if he is the village idiot and knows nothing about things that any native twelve-year-old can tell you all about! In short, deceptive, but a good try.

Apart from the situations themselves the language used in them should be presented in a recognizable format. A distinction has to be made between texts 'written to be read' and texts 'spoken to be heard'. Such a distinction, and more refined ones, have consequences for textbook presentation. We expect advertisements to be offered in a certain way, and this is different from a newspaper editorial, which is different from the way the newspaper presents an accident report, and this is different from the description of an accident in a short story, or a novel, and so on. Is it really necessary to present a letter in a written format, like the following?

5.1 *A letter to Anwar*
It's eight-thirty in the evening, Karim is sitting in his room, writing his first letter to his cousin Anwar in Bombay, a big city in India.

99b St. Stephen's Gardens
London W2
England

Dear Anwar,
I'm writing to you in English because I can't write Urdu, our language. My Father and Mother and my brother Hossein and my sister Sheree can speak and write Urdu, but I can't. I can understand it.
I can speak a bit of French because we're learning it at school this year. In my class we are reading a magazine called 'Bonjour les copains'. It's about six children in Paris. What languages are you learning at school this year? What languages can you speak?
(...)
Well, until next time. Love to uncle Ayub and Auntie.

Yours, Karim

(Huub Rutten and Frank van Ruyssevelt, *Notting Hill Gate*, Textbook 1, p44, 1986. 's Hertogenbosch, Netherlands: Malmberg)

One of the attractive features of this textbook is that it deals with immigrants from a variety of former British colonies. They live their lives, have contacts with each other, in the area of London called Notting Hill Gate, and some get on well with each other, while others do not. The texts, on the whole, manage to involve Dutch learners, since they deal with topics they recognize as interesting and close to their own experience. The above letter is on the whole reasonably convincing, although, as it is the first of its kind, why doesn't Karim introduce himself? The problem he mentions of not being able to write Urdu, however, is one that many children born in immigrant families would recognize.

One of the first requirements of reading and listening materials is that texts are authentic, ie obey the rules of discourse as agreed by native speakers (cf. McCarthy 1991; McCarthy and Carter 1993). For teaching purposes there is a further requirement, namely that they represent actual language use of native speakers in a context the learners find recognizable and useful. Authenticity involves more than just the presentation of text. Quite often learners have a problem recognizing the relevance of the situation offered for their edification. What they need is communication situations they recognize as relevant, ie learners recognize that they might have to fend for themselves in situations like 'going shopping', 'having to buy a train ticket', 'asking the way', and so on.

One area that many textbook writers generally do not touch on is culture in its widest sense. Why not introduce a learner of English and have him/her explain a common phenomenon of his/her native culture to an English, or other foreign, contemporary? Topics might be: items of food typical of the home culture, customary ways of dealing with everyday occurrences like meal times, visiting people at home, etc.

Many language teachers are afraid of such settings because they have picked up the notion that learners must not be confronted with errors. These will be copied by the learners thus leading to problems in the future and difficulties with getting rid of them. This is clearly a left-over from the days of 'drill or kill' teaching. Learners will recognize the setting and realize that a non-native user of English will make mistakes when trying to get the message across. There is no reason why the teacher should not ask the class if they could improve on the original.

Part of our language competence consists in the ability to recognize text types, and adjust our reactions accordingly. Similarly, in spoken texts: a journalist's report of a football match will sound different during the match from the summary by the same reporter after the match, which will be different in style from a report on the latest summit meeting of the presidents of the seven most important industrial nations, which is different from an interview, which is different from a talk show, and so on. In other words, texts that are written to be read should be recognizable, and offered, as such. And texts spoken to be heard should not be in the textbook as reading texts, unless we are dealing with drama, where possible interpretations of a text are worked out on the basis of printed dialogues.

Activity 5.8 What about the following text? Would you consider it acceptable, ie 'authentic' in the double sense explained above?

Luton people say No to foreign languages

by our correspondent

Luton College students asked people in the town centre on Saturday morning about their feelings about foreign languages. Only 8% of Luton people say they can speak a European foreign language.

They asked people if they were sorry they could only speak English. A common reaction was: 'Well, everybody speaks English on the continent, so it doesn't matter.'

People from other backgrounds often spoke other languages than English at home, of course.

(John Strange *et al. Friends, International English*, p31. Houten: Educaboek 1994)

In the textbook it is presented as a newspaper item, although it was 'invented' by the authors of the textbook.[8]

This does not mean that textbook writers must only use text taken from real sources, as they were actually produced at a given time. There is no reason why they should not invent situations and dialogues to fit them: the only condition is that native speakers recognize them as the real thing: 'This is how it could have been written or said by a native in this setting!'

Activity 5.9 Collect a number of textbooks, say four, two produced abroad and two in your own country, intended for any level, and judge the texts for authenticity, as discussed above.[9]

These days there is no reason why texts should only be presented in a printed and/or in an audio format. Video has been around for many years now and could be enormously helpful in the presentation of communication settings, particularly when cultural misunderstandings, or just differences, and how to cope with them, is the topic of study. CD-i and CD-ROM have similar advantages, particularly in the context of private study sessions, but at present are still in a stage of development.

Checks on comprehension

There is a wide variety of exercise types available to check on the understanding of texts, both listening and reading. These vary from pre-reading (and pre-listening) activities to checks of global understanding, of understanding of details, of awareness-raising questions, and many others. The following is an example of such an exercise accompanying a listening activity.

IAN'S DAY

Complete Ian's responses:

I work at ____________________
I normally ____________________
The first thing we do ____________________
And then we usually ____________________

> Why does Ian like his job?
> What doesn't he like about it?
> What does he think is his strongest point?

(Anneli Luukas and Joan Nordlund, *Challenge, English for Communication*, Helsingissä Kustannusosakeyhtiö Otava 1994, textbook p27)

This sort of activity can be organized in many ways. The most productive is probably to allow the class, in small groups, to negotiate the best answers to the questions, perhaps beginning with individual attempts and in steps building up towards whole-class agreement.

A problem with some types of checking activities is that basically they are tests, and are recognized as such by learners. A serious problem may be that it is hard to convince the learners of the continuing necessity of such tasks, once they have got the message of the text presented. The solution must lie in linking this sort of activity with a 'task' the learner is to perform at the end of the learning unit. Having established this task, hopefully presented in the textbook, the relevance of exercises as a preparation for the performance of the task should be obvious. The requirements of the task are projected back on to the exercises, so to speak. If the unit is concerned with 'buying tickets' (for a journey, for a cinema, for a theatre, etc), there are things the learners need to know. Apart from certain phrases and words to refer to what it is they want, to ask the price, and so on, they may need to be aware of the correct tone of voice for such occasions. Too polite, and they will create misunderstanding. If the wrong code is used, they will be understood as being sarcastic, perhaps. (How would you feel, if you were just expected to sell entrance tickets, and someone addressed you with: 'Excuse me for interrupting your work, but could you possibly find a moment to sell me two adults' and three children's admission tickets to the fair?') This sort of mismatch between language, situation and speaker should always be avoided.

The type of activity we are looking for then, goes beyond the level of checking if the learner 'knows the facts of the situation', but checks on 'growing awareness' of what is suitable language use in this context in terms of role relationships between interlocutors. What is also needed, of course, is the means to obtain information we have missed or misunderstood: phrases to compensate for lack of what the situation requires in terms of language.

Activity 5.10 As a result of the previous exercise you should now have some authentic texts. Now look at the activities checking on the learners' comprehension of these. Are they sufficiently authentic? Are they linked to the performance of a task later in the unit? Do they ask for 'facts' only? Do they attempt to increase awareness of appropriateness of language use?[10]

Developing skills

This part of the textbook unit generally receives plenty of attention from writers. This is where structural exercises find a place, vocabulary training gets attention, pronunciation is dealt with, etc. There is obviously a great deal to be done in developing the various areas of the language skills which allow learners to communicate properly in the foreign language.

The danger is always present, and often insufficiently avoided, that learners are only asked to perform tricks and not required to work towards meaningful communication. The rubric: 'Rewrite the following sentences in ...' (past tense, passive voice, simple present, etc), is much too familiar and, as every teacher knows, is generally an efficient time killer, but contributes nothing to motivating the learners.

Again we would hope to find reference to the performance of a task with an indication of what this means in terms of 'correctness and appropriacy of language'. The learner would thus know what would be required to perform the task properly.

Activity 5.11 In the previous two activities you have critically judged some recent EFL teaching materials. Select an English language teaching unit which fulfils the conditions we have set so far. Analyse this unit, assigning exercises to the various sub-skills, spelling, syntax, pronunciation, intonation, areas of pragmatics and discourse, etc, receiving attention, and relate these to the task set in the unit. Do they fit?[11]

Controlled practice

What about the following?

The following dialogue is between a clerk in a travel agency and a woman customer. Make all the changes necessary to produce, from the notes below, a complete dialogue. The first sentence has been done for you as an example.

CLERK: I/help/you > *May I help you?*
WOMAN: Yes/I/like/book flight/Rio.
1 ....
CLERK: When/you intend/travel?
2 ....?
WOMAN: As soon/possible. No later/end/this week.
3 ....
CLERK: Well/that/be/difficult/this time/year unless/you be very lucky.
4 ....
WOMAN: But/it be/absolutely/essential/I/get there/end/this week!
5 ....!
CLERK: All right/I/do/what/I/can. You like/sit down?
6 ....?
WOMAN: No/I/be/back/half an hour.
7 ....
CLERK: All right/I/probably/know/then./I/have/your name?
8 ....?

(Robert O'Neill: *Success at First Certificate*, p117. Oxford University Press 1987)

Adults will probably recognize the situation as relevant for their future as a tourist. However, would they book a journey in English? In my experience a tourist looks up a travel agent's to confirm a return booking, or change it, perhaps to complain about something in his/her present arrangements, but rarely to arrange a trip to another country from Britain, except perhaps when he/she has missed a connection. Also, the dialogue allows no room for individual creative use of language, nor, unfortunately, for the development of compensatory strategies. What should we do to solve the problem?

The type of exercise needed for 'controlled practice' must reflect the performance of the task insofar as the learner is allowed freedom to choose the actual words and phrasing needed for the exercise. That freedom to choose, however, is restricted by the information offered about things like context, interlocutor, setting and development of the communication up to this moment.

Say and write

Captain Blake's Story

It (be) in December 1945. We (arrive) in Bermuda and then (sail) towards Florida. Five planes (circle) above us. We (watch) them: It (be) very strange. Everything (be) wrong. Then the spaceship (arrive). The planes (stop) and our boat (stop) too. The spaceship (move) above the planes and above us. Then the planes (disappear). The boat (disappear). Only the spaceship (be) there. Who was I? Where was I ...? The answers (not be) clear. Then the rescue planes (arrive). I (be) in the sea. They (search) for the five planes and they (search) for my boat, but they (not be) successful.

Say
Now interview Captain Blake for television! Use *when, where, what, did, was, were,* etc.

A *When did you arrive in Bermuda, Captain Blake?*
B *I (we) arrived in December 1945.*

(Jon Blundell, *English Visa*, Student's Book 1 p34. Oxford University Press)

This activity allows to some extent for individual freedom and creativity, in that both the interviewer and Captain Blake can develop the dialogue using the information given in the preceding text. But what is actually said depends on how the interviewer structures the interview. Another problem might well be that not many learners will recognize themselves in the role of TV talk show personality.

The question of what level of language command may be expected is of a different level. Dealing with the past tense forms of regular verbs (except *be*) mostly occurs fairly early on in the course, and consequently this activity might at this stage be somewhat beyond the command of the learners. To some extent this problem may be circumvented by preparing the interview in groups and asking two members to present their final product to the class.

An important aspect of this type of learning activity is: reflection on the actual choices made by the learner and the reasons for making them. It is not enough to assign 'right' or 'wrong' to individual utterances, because it does not help the learning process along, at least not sufficiently. Obviously, the amount of freedom of choice may vary according to the authors' estimate of what the learner can be expected to do at this juncture in the course.

Activity 5.12 Take a recent EFL textbook, and judge some 'controlled practice' activities on their authenticity as exercises, as discussed above, taking into account the quality of the information provided in the textbook/workbook, and the amount and quality of reflection demanded. What does the learner take away from it? How much 'involvement' is expected?[12]

Quality of the task

So far I have left the definition of 'task' rather vague. It is supposed to show a relationship with the objectives of the course and it should be recognizably authentic to both learner and native speaker. Here we ought to be more precise, if possible.

The following game is of a very popular type produced in the 1980s. It allows the people taking part to show off their ability to use English to their advantage:

GAME
'Shipwrecked'. Imagine that you have been shipwrecked. Six people have survived but there is only room for four people in the lifeboat. Work in groups of six. You must each think of reasons why *you* should have a place in the boat and the others be thrown into the sea! (*Or* each member chooses to be a famous person and must explain why their person should survive.) Then tell the other members of the group. Finally you should all vote to decide who has the best reasons for surviving!

One of the problems in language classes is that the number of occasions when English is spoken just for communication is limited, even when drama and/or roleplay activities are a regular ingredient of the language lessons. So, any opportunity to allow learners to use the language as best they can should be welcomed. Unfortunately, it has been my experience quite often that learners felt no affinity with the situation of being shipwrecked and could not honestly take it seriously.

Language teaching/learning objectives nowadays are stated in terms of the ability to perform adequately, appropriately and up to a point correctly in certain, stated, communication situations. Such situations can be broken down into sub-situations, representing possible alternatives, a number of sub-units, each contributing to the whole, and a number of alternative routes leading to closure of the communication situation.

Sub-situations are easiest illustrated with an example. In the situation 'buying and selling' a sub-situation would be 'buying something in a bakery'. Another one would be 'buying something at the greengrocer's', or 'buying something in a bakery where the personnel know you'.

Sub-units may be the setting: the physical surroundings of the communication situation; the roles: the relationships between the various actors in the setting: age, educational background, temperament, mood, sex, group membership, different cultural backgrounds and so on; and the topic: the problem to be solved, the agreement to be reached, etc. The bakery, to go back to the example in the previous paragraph, might be a small one in a local neighbourhood, or a big one in a shopping centre, or a stall in the market place. In the bakery one might be served by the baker's wife or one of the counter staff, or by the baker himself, or ... Perhaps we might even include 'social chat' as a possibility, if the customer is familiar. The topic may be buying a loaf, or a cake, or biscuits, in short anything the shop offers its customers, or even something available from bakers in the native country but not abroad.

Alternative routes, if we stick to the baker's shop, may be represented by variations in quantity, non-availability of an item wanted, suggested alternatives, and so on.

Each of the sub-situations may be combined with variations in sub-units and alternative routes to provide the teacher with a large number of possible tasks. Some of these may be relatively easy, others will require much more competence on the part of the learner. Ordering these according to difficulty makes it possible to do a proper job of selecting and grading, thus giving the learner the opportunity to show that for the execution of this particular task he/she has acquired competence as to when to speak, when not, and as to what to talk about with whom, when, where, and in what manner.

Activity 5.13 Have a look at some tasks in a collection of roleplay activities. (See note 13 for a few titles, if needed.) Decide on their authenticity and their usefulness with a group of learners you are familiar with. What competencies would be needed to perform these tasks properly?[13]

Developing intercultural understanding

So far most textbooks for the European EFL market have mainly concerned themselves with understanding British culture, providing information on a variety of topics to do with the way society is organized. Sometimes reference is made to the USA, but the rest of the English-speaking world is ignored. Familiar topics, such as 'driving on the left', 'school uniforms', 'attitude to sports', etc, are mentioned, but only rarely does one come across a first-hand experience of direct confrontation with things being done differently in Britain. Textbooks do sometimes offer an opportunity to learners to provide information to a British visitor on the locality in which they live. This type of activity might be extended to include the use of English as a lingua franca, of course.

The classroom offers a place where pupils may compare intercultural experiences. A great deal of language learning takes place outside the classroom, even if it is initiated inside. The media, in particular, offer widespread exposure to written and spoken language, which helps to develop linguistic competence enormously. Every language teacher should encourage learners to watch TV shows broadcast in English and read books in English at home and at leisure. The great advantage of such activities lies in a stress-free setting, which in turn leads to a much better return for the time invested.

The most widely used form of time investment is still in encouraging reading. Most learners enjoy the occasional good book. And popular books, as we all know, reflect the cultural norms and values of their readers (cf. Rönnqvist and Sell 1994). Therefore, foreign language teachers should invest much time in encouraging the reading habit in their learners. A well-stocked library is in itself no guarantee for enthusiasm among its users. Reading projects may help a great deal, particularly those that manage to catch the interest of the pupils.

Developing good reading habits depends to a very large extent on developing learners' awareness of what they are doing right and what they are doing wrong, which in turn depends on awareness on the part of the teacher of what learners are doing and what can be done to improve the learners' approach to reading. Several helpful suggestions for teachers can be found for example in *Learning to Learn English*. (See the suggestions for further study at the end of this chapter.)

Newspaper projects can provide learners with lots of information about the foreign culture. Activities can vary from: 'What news items receive the most attention in the British press?' to 'How do the British present this particular issue in the press?' If colleagues teaching other foreign languages, and other subjects as well naturally, are interested, the project might include the reading of a selection of international newspapers in a variety of languages. News in one's own country, issues receiving a lot of coverage in the national press, may hardly appear abroad, and vice versa, of course.

Activity 5.14 What international issue is currently being widely debated in the national press? How is it presented? Look up how this matter is treated in a number of foreign newspapers, including *The European* or another news publication, or TV news broadcast (CNN, for example), aimed at an international audience. In what respects is the presentation similar or different?[14]

Direct experience with British culture, let alone with any of the other English-speaking cultures at classroom level, is not always easy to organize. The cost of travel and accommodation makes regular school visits to Britain difficult, but a good alternative is possible through watching a popular TV serial, or organizing an E-mail (Electronic mail) exchange, or a class correspondence project. The learners will make several discoveries, of course. Some of these are to be expected, but some may need a little push on the part of the teacher, particularly when the class textbook is along traditional lines and barely gives meaning its due in relation to structure. This may lead to important discoveries for the learner in the field of pragmatics, the way people organize relationships between participants in the conversation during the exchange and negotiation of meaning.

TV viewing projects are not all that difficult to arrange these days, although in some countries it may be difficult to watch programmes in English, since these are habitually dubbed. One possibility may be using cable or satellite TV. Apart from these difficulties, not every learner may be able to watch a particular channel at the agreed time, for any number of reasons. Hence the most advisable approach is to invest time in collecting topical materials as they are broadcast and arrange to view these whenever the learners have time. Fortunately many publishers bring out viewing materials which are not linked to a particular coursebook. (Tomalin and Stempleski 1993 offer many interesting and useful suggestions.) The same applies to listening materials, which may well be cheaper to get hold of. In due course, CD-i and CD-ROM materials will become available, making it possible for individual learners to communicate actively with a computer programme.

Much more rewarding, not least because of the amount of enthusiasm generated among learners, are projects which link learners with colleagues abroad. Several possibilities have been tried out and published in language teaching publications. Recently a secondary school in Arnhem gained a prize for a correspondence project in which pupils exchanged letters with a group of Airborne Veterans who had taken part in the Battle of Arnhem in 1944.

It is not always necessary to arrange for a link with an English-speaking country. A link with a group of learners having comparable communication problems in the foreign language to your own pupils could probably be even more rewarding. Such a link emphasizes the use of English as a lingua franca, and may help learners discover and solve the problems of communication with a foreign culture other than the ones they are, more or less, familiar with.

Teachers have experimented with Telex, with E-Mail, with video links and audio links and, of course, with ordinary letters, sent by post. Some even use the Internet for the exchange of information and letters. Each has its obvious advantages and disadvantages. One is faster, another provides visual clues which show up cultural differences much more clearly than print does, and many more. The main advantage of these over visits abroad is that they are relatively cheap, and certainly cost much less than travelling to a foreign town, even if the school provides accommodation for the visiting pupils and staff. However, if a visit has been prepared through exchanges of letters of one kind or another pupils will be mutually interested in a meeting with their correspondents from abroad. Arranging for exchanges of learners between two countries can be very satisfying, but they do require a solid investment in time, and perhaps money as well.

Activity 5.15 You have probably visited Great Britain more than just once or twice. Do you remember your first visit? What did you learn while you were staying there that you didn't know before? Are your experiences of that time in any way comparable to your learners' experiences now?[15]

Many of the activities discussed above can be done with learners at different levels of language competence. For beginners and lower intermediate learners one has to be careful to offer activities they can command. For those learners who have achieved a higher level of competence in the foreign language it is possible to decide on a much wider range of activities. Some have been mentioned above, such as newspaper and video projects, but it is certainly possible to carry out 'research' using readily accessible sources. 'Humour' is an interesting field of study (Riley 1989b). Cartoons carry all sorts of cultural overtones, which may be interesting to discover. Different cultures do have a different perception of what is funny, and what is not. There may even be important differences between cultures which use the same native language.

Literature can be a rich field for the discovery of cultural differences. One might ask learners to draw up a list of what parents require of their children as they grow up. The list should then be illustrated on the basis of extracts from books they have read. One important question is of course whether what is portrayed in the book is accepted by the social group represented in the context offered by the author.

Another possibility might be to collect examples of exchanges of lingua franca use of English and analyse these not so much for actual mistakes in the use of grammar or vocabulary, but for misunderstandings caused by cultural differences. Gerard Willems provided me with the following example of a dialogue between a Dutch and a French academic who were on the same plane on their way home from an international conference in Italy. The Dutchman is much younger than the Frenchman, who has a rather 'academic' bearing. The speakers have seen each other at the conference, but not spoken to each other. On taking their seats on the plane they find that they are next to each other. A is Dutch and B is French.

A: Hello! Erm ... have you seat B or the window seat?
B: Bonjour, eum ... I have to er ... look. Er ... the window seat.
(They install themselves)
A: What a coincidence that we should sit next to each other!
B: Yes, eum ... what a coincidence.
A: What did you think of the conference?
B: Well erm ... it was alright.
A: I was quite surprised you know by the efficiency of the organization. I had expected something a bit more erm ... how shall I put it erm ... a bit more erm ... well chaotic is too strong a word but erm ...
B: I do not understand what you want to say ...
A: Well, you know, there is this European joke about Europe being sheer hell if all the cooks come from Britain, all the erm ... civil servants from Germany, all the policemen from France ...
B: I do not like ... such jokes ...
A: Well, anyway it ends with that everything there is organized by the Italians ...
B: That is all stereotypes. Excuse me eum ...
A: I talked to other participants and some said the Italians are very careful when they organize something and do you think French share with the Italians that you want to organize well, you leave nothing to chance, want to make sure ... erm ...?

B: Well you have ... eum ... need of some chance if you organize something big like this congress. Tant de choses peuvent ...
A: I don't understand, ...
B: Oh, excusez-moi ...
A: ... No, no, not the French but you said you need chance ...
B: You see, eum ... my English is not so good.
A: No, I think I misunderstood, 'leaving to chance' means not to take risks ...
B: You must excuse me, I cannot follow ... (searches in his bag for something)
A: Well, I see you have other things to do ...

Willems's comments on the behaviour between the two are that the Dutchman 'does not make an attempt to create a context for negotiation in a sufficiently open way. He seems to think that having seen each other at the same conference provides enough shared background and context to build on in the way he did. He does not take into account that the Frenchman, being older, may expect a little more respect for his seniority from a younger colleague even if he happens to be a foreign fellow-traveller. The Dutch egalitarian culture with its small power distance is what strikes a lot of French people as difficult to live with.' (Willems 1995)

A follow-up activity might well be, he suggests, to rewrite this dialogue adding to and correcting the discourse mistakes of the two speakers. The Dutchman should show more respect to the Frenchman, eg by asking if it is all right to speak English, by being less direct in bringing up stereotypical views of other cultures, by using phrases that help to create openness and by suspending judgement. Such an activity will obviously help even advanced learners to become more alert and circumspect in their dealings with representatives of other cultures.

Obviously, the better the command of the foreign language in the group of learners the more ambitious can be the project agreed with them, within the context of course requirements.

Testing language competence

The testing of linguistic competence still suffers from the sins of its past. When 'objective testing' became fashionable in educational circles, in the 1960s, testing language command proved problematical. It turned out to be possible to test the so-called receptive skills in isolation, which led to the development of objective tests of reading comprehension and listening comprehension. Testing the productive skills, by means of objective tests, led to results that were considered ridiculous, mainly because language teachers felt the test formats bore no relationship to what was required of speakers and writers using language. What remains from this time is the idea that it is possible to test the individual sub-skills, such as spelling or pronunciation, that make up the total skill, and add up the results, thus achieving a scientific assessment of a person's linguistic competence.

The problem with this solution was, and is, that it is possible to describe a number of sub-skills quite scientifically and objectively, but there always turns out to be something else involved in language production, not covered in the various tests, such as 'body language' or 'rules of text presentation'. In short, we are up against something like an integrated competence. Apart from this, there is the difficulty of weighting the sub-skills which make up the whole. And if the experts cannot agree, what is the poor language teacher to do? To make matters even worse, researchers in the field of language acquisition have shown that there need not be a direct relationship between a person's grammatical competence as shown in a grammar test and this same person's grammatical performance in actual production, both spoken and written. (Tarone 1988 Chapter 3)

Nobody is particularly happy with the conclusion, which seems almost inescapable, that one cannot test linguistic competence in an objective manner. ('Objective' in this context meaning that assessing the results of a particular test requires no specialist knowledge, and can in fact be done by a machine. Setting the questions remains, of course, a task for the experts!)

One of the solutions, that pupils assess their performance themselves, has been worked into at least one textbook. Learners do their activity and are then asked to fill in their Task Form, which may subsequently be discussed in class. The format is quite simple and straightforward:

1 Did you think this activity was important?
2 Did you speak English only?
3 Did your partner understand you?
4 Did you finish the task successfully?

Name three things you have learnt in this Part. You can answer in Dutch.
1 ....
2 ....
3 ....

(John Strange *et al. Friends, International English*, Workbook 1. Houten: Educaboek 1994)

It is a way out of the problem to some extent; the advantage is that learners are no longer subjected to stress, because they do not know what is coming. They do the 'task' to prove to themselves, and to their teacher, that they can do it. But it does only partly solve the teacher's problem. In the old-fashioned classroom the teacher cannot but fall back on subjective assessment, a very 'unscientific' approach to judging a person's competence to deal with the intricacies of a particular communication problem. One way out is to follow the traditional advice: 'The proof of the pudding is in the eating.' If you are in doubt whether someone can 'eat foreign language pudding', put one in front of him/her and watch what he/she makes of it.

Assessing the results of oral proficiency tests, and writing proficiency tests, has to be done differently, if objective assessment is impossible. The solution has been found in organizing 'scoring teams'. This means assessment by jury, which is a time-consuming business, but works. It is not a perfect solution, since different people tend to value different aspects of communication and may therefore come up with different scores. However, this problem can be solved by providing a scoring team with sufficient training, involving sessions where the members of the team are asked to score a number of tests individually, then compare and discuss their marks, score a further number of tests and discuss these, until a reasonable amount of agreement (inter-scorer reliability) has been achieved. Such teams work reasonably well and, if they regularly attend rehearsal sessions, continue to produce reliable results.

Let us return to the problem of assessment of the individual performance of communication tasks. There is now a solution available to the difficulty of judging the productive skills: setting up scoring teams. The next problem is organizing communication tasks in such a manner that the way an individual learner solves a particular task can be compared with what another learner does. Again, there is no easy solution. For writing, it is possible to give the same test paper to a large group. Setting the same oral production task to a group of 25 people who all have to wait their turn to show that they can do it is asking for various sorts of trouble. For practical reasons it is therefore necessary to devise comparable sets of communication tasks, using complex pictures, for example, with or without the support of key words, and give these out to individuals, at the same time seeing to it that the product each task leads to can be compared with the others.

Activity 5.16 Devise a set of different tasks you could use with a group of lower-intermediate level learners around the topic of 'Going shopping for something to eat'. How are you going to assess individual performance of the tasks? What will be your instructions to judges concerning features of linguistic and intercultural competence? What extra equipment will you need?[16]

Conclusion

The international discussion about learning languages for international communication has been going on for some twenty years now, if not longer. It is an issue that should greatly concern the practising language teacher. The problem seems to be that policy makers have not yet made up their minds about the importance of preparing the school population for the changed world they will meet when they have left school.

Solutions to the problem have been discussed widely, and are available for any teachers who need them. This book will, I hope, help teachers to find ways towards solving some of the problems posed by the multicultural classroom, and will have pointed the way towards some of the literature on the subject.

Notes

1 This activity is useful for people who have little experience with languages other than their own. For trainee teachers it might be turned into a small research project, particularly if the group happens to be mainly from the same cultural background, by setting the task of consulting a number of grammars of exotic and familiar languages. Japanese and Arabic, for example, have the same word categories but use a different ordering: actor – object – action, and action – actor – object, respectively.

2 If you use this activity with trainees, I suggest that you select a number of grammar points from the list provided in the previous sections. However, if this activity is done in a truly multicultural setting, oral interaction about these and similar possible areas of learning difficulty will bring on lots of discussion and many intriguing discoveries (eg comparison with so-called agglutinating languages). Allow enough time for the presentation of various findings.

3 One discovery likely to be made is the way the basic meaning is organized. *Book*, for example, is defined as *a bundle of papers for reading or for writing*, plus a few meanings derived from this first meaning. One dictionary combines these into one definition, whereas others keep the two apart. Also, dictionaries differ in the number of 'extra' contexts offered, etc. Personal associations will perhaps be with one particular book you were very fond of, or a regular occasion in which a book played an important role for you, such as father reading your favourite book to you before you had to go to sleep, or father reading a chapter from the Bible, or another religious book, after dinner, when you wanted to go out and play, and many, many others.

4 The differences have to do with the way societies are organized. Cultural differences become apparent in the way 'shared' meanings belong to a word. This may be a useful activity to do with trainees, perhaps also with upper intermediate and advanced learners of English.

5 This type of activity is valuable for students as well as trainees, as it makes areas of misunderstanding more transparent. If you use a direct translation of a phrase in your language in a conversation with a native speaker of English, who may not be familiar with other languages, the chances are you are impolite, rude or even worse. Willems (1993a) relates the following incident: 'A French holidaymaker wheeling his trolley around a supermarket in an English town accidentally crashes into another trolley pushed by a local woman. In keeping with what he would do in France he utters what he thinks is an apology: 'Excuse me!' He is subsequently completely taken aback by the English woman's reaction to a companion: 'I don't know! They just charge around without looking and do not even apologize!' What he did not know was that what he uttered had the function of asking the woman to make way for him, and that in order to apologize he should have said: 'Oh, I am so/awfully/terribly sorry.' (Riley, oral communication in Willems 1993a section 3.1). The text contains more examples and a discussion of a variety of types of pragmatic, discoursal and strategic errors. Many useful insights may also be found in Kasper 1986.

6 Many of the non-verbal signals mankind uses are not culture specific but are part of our natural heritage. Desmond Morris has made an extensive study of signs man uses in communication: intentional and non-intentional, conscious and unconscious (Desmond Morris, *Manwatching*, Jonathan Cape London 1977). Misunderstandings occur when non-verbal signals mean different things in different cultures, like the Dutch sign to the barman for two beers which in a similar British setting is an affront and may be interpreted as a slur on the quality of service or the quality of the beer – at any rate is unacceptable behaviour.

7 This 'invented' dialogue, on the basis of a Russian source pointed out to me by G Stoks (National Institute for Curriculum Development, Enschede, Netherlands), suffers from far too many shortcomings. Setting, topic and roles are undefinable. Assuming that this conversation is between a mother and child, no British mother would use phrases like these, neither would any normal English child. Make the mother an au pair girl who does not speak English very well, and even then an interpretation where John is using irony to put her in her place won't work. The most gracious explanation for offering this type of text might be that it illustrates the use of some prepositions, but even so ...

8 The text is intended to be dealt with as 'text written to be read'. On the whole it does show characteristics of that type of newspaper report of a research project, but in one or two instances the language is perhaps too simple: two sentences where the journalist would have combined them into one, with main and sub-clause, and simple words like *asked* and *say* in the first few sentences, where the journalist would perhaps have preferred *questioned* or *interviewed* and *admit*. However, this is from Book 1 of the course and is intended for first-form learners in secondary education in the Netherlands (who have had some experience of learning English in the last years of Primary School).

9 The activity may be useful to do with EFL teacher trainees.

One discovery may be that texts do mainly portray English as used by average middle class Standard British English speakers: adult parents with two children, a boy and a girl, a house of their own, a family car, a dog, and, of course, an above average income. Britain is not really like that at all, as we know. One result of having been taught English from this type of coursebook may be that youngsters from a working-class background end up speaking a high-brow variety of British English, which has a ludicrous effect on native speakers of a comparable background (Pygmalion effect). Textbooks could include examples of English as used by people from the Midlands, or Scotland, or Wales, to name a few. They might offer examples of English as used by non-native speakers, West Indians or Pakistanis. This would be appropriately authentic, surely.

10 The point of this activity is the 'authenticity' of the task set in the exercise. Is this what the reader/listener would normally do to comprehend the text? If the text illustrates language as used in a setting that the learners will be asked to cope with, the exercise should draw attention to features of the text that may be useful to know about later on. Does the activity do both? Excellent, but it may not be relevant to require both from the exercise to hand.

11 The chances are that the more recent materials will meet the requirement of exercises and other learning activities being related to the performance of a task at the end of the unit. A great many textbooks for English in my country claim to work towards developing communicative competence, but tend to forget the meaning of 'communicative' or seem to understand it as referring to 'grammatical' competence.

12 The type of learning activity under this rubric would typically be a preparation for the performance of the task at the end of the unit. It should draw attention to strategies involved in doing the exercise, pragmatic and discoursal pitfalls, and perhaps draw attention to errors caused by cultural differences, etc. Then it should offer an activity which clearly states the limitations set by setting, topic and roles.

13 There are many collections of roleplay activities available for English. To mention only a few, without any pretence at completeness: David Norman, Ulf Levihn and Jan Anders Hedenquist, *Communicative Ideas*, Language Teaching Publications 1986; Alan Maley and Alan Duff, *Drama Techniques in Language Teaching*, Cambridge University Press 1982; Friederike Klippel, *Keep Talking*, Cambridge University Press 1984; Penny Ur, *Discussions that Work*, Cambridge University Press 1981; Andrew Wright, David Betteridge and Michael Buckby, *Games for Language Learning*, Cambridge University Press 1979; Pat Pattison, *Developing Communication Skills*, Cambridge University Press 1987.

More background information may be found in Michael Legutke and Howard Thomas, *Process and Experience in the Language Classroom*, Longman Group 1991, in particular in Chapters 3 and 4.

14 This is an activity that might work extremely well in the upper forms of secondary education, particularly if an item can be found that will be of interest to the learners. As to procedure, I would suggest organizing the project as groupwork. Each group, after a general discussion of issues and ways of finding solutions, etc, makes up its own programme of points they would like to clear up, collects the materials and sources they wish to consult and reports back to the class at an agreed time.

15 The difference will probably be mainly a difference in time, in the sense that even British society has changed over the years and other issues have come to occupy the public mind, compared to the first time you were there. If you use this activity with trainees, it is my experience that they are keenly interested in hearing stories from your first visit; as interested as you are in hearing their experiences.

16 A helpful solution may be to draw up a number of shopping lists (perhaps in the learner's native language?), including one or two items which are common in your own culture, but perhaps not in Britain. These last will require the use of compensatory strategies (see Chapter 3, *Objectives for language learning*), of course. The assessment might take account of the use of discourse rules, polite phrasing of certain types of requests, opening and closing of the discourse, etc. Clearly one useful check would be whether the learner has managed to get hold of every item on the list. If you work with a jury, you need recording equipment; cassette-recorders may be sufficient, but in order to catch body language and facial expression you might find it helpful to record the activities on video.

Suggestions for further study

The British Council has been very active in the field of issues in language teaching. On a fairly regular basis they organize small-scale conferences and publish the papers read on that occasion. One of these deals with intercultural language teaching. The publication is: Brian Harrison (ed.), *Culture and the Language Classroom*, ELT Documents, Modern English Publications 1990.

The training of language teachers still occupies the attention of the Council of Europe's team of experts. This has resulted in: Henry G Widdowson, *A Rationale for Language Teacher Education*, Strasbourg 1987.

The language classroom and the issue of materials for intercultural education has been widely studied and has led to some very useful publications, among them Gerhard Neuner, *A Socio-cultural Framework for Communicative Teaching and Learning of Foreign Languages at the School Level*, Strasbourg 1988.

In this chapter I have used the framework developed in Germany following the publication of the *Hessische Rahmenrichtlinien*. An English version was published in 1981: Christopher Candlin (ed.), *The Communicative Teaching of English, Principles and an Exercise Typology*, Longman, London 1981. The difficulty with this, and other exercise typologies, is that there is no assessment of the 'effect' of the exercise discussed on the quality of learning. The Council of Europe have also published a very useful analysis and discussion of exercise types with a commentary: Joe Sheils, *Communication in the Modern Languages Classroom*, Strasbourg 1988.

The issue of language testing has received attention in a large number of publications of the Council of Europe, eg V Kohonen *et al.*, *Evaluation and Testing in the Learning and Teaching of Languages for Communication*, Strasbourg 1988. Of very practical value is: Peter S Green (ed.), *Communicative Language Testing, A Resource Handbook for Teacher Trainers*, Strasbourg 1987. Another interesting publication is: M Oskarsson, *Approaches to Self-assessment in Foreign Language Learning*, Pergamon Press 1978.

Self-directed learning is an important area of development in the field of language teaching. The first was H Holec, *Autonomy and Foreign Language Learning*, Strasbourg 1980, a discussion of the concept plus reports of a few attempts at getting the idea off the ground. In 1988 a survey was published of trials, some very successful, in various member countries of the Council of Europe: H Holec, *Autonomy and Self-directed Learning: Present Fields of Application*, Strasbourg 1988. ELT Documents 131, edited by Arthur Brookes and Peter Grundy, deals with *Individualisation and Autonomy in Language Learning* (Modern English Publications in association with The British Council 1988) in a number of different settings. Gail Ellis and Barbara Sinclair, *Learning to Learn English*, (Cambridge University Press 1989) is probably more accessible. A slightly wider scope is set up in Susan Sheerin, *Self-access*, Oxford University Press 1989, which discusses the conditions to be met in setting up a learning centre mainly, but not only, for adult learners.

Larry E. Smith (ed.) *Discourse Across Cultures*, Prentice Hall International 1987, provides background material for teaching and learning languages for international communication. The area of discourse analysis has seen a large number of publications dealing with this field. I have found Michael McCarthy, *Discourse Analysis for Language Teachers* (Cambridge University Press 1991) very useful, and the same must be said of Evelyn Hatch, *Discourse and Language Education* (Cambridge University Press 1992).

A recent publication which explicitly pays attention to coming to grips with other cultures in classroom activities is Rob Nolasco and Lois Arthur, *Conversation*, Oxford University Press 1987, and, of course, the even more recent book by Barry Tomalin and Susan Stempleski, *Cultural Awareness*, Oxford University Press 1993.

Many other compilations of language activity materials can be used for the purpose of developing learner autonomy, but will need some conscious attention and preparation on the part of the teacher. An interesting book in this context is Colin Campbell and Hanna Kryszewska, *Learner-based Teaching*, Oxford University Press 1992.

Bibliography

Adams, D. 1993 *Mostly Harmless* p113. London: Pan Books

Aitchison, J. 1981 *Language Change: Progress or Decay.* London: Fontana Paperbacks

Alix, C. and Kodron, C. 1988 *Zusammenarbeiten: Gemeinsames Lernen. Office Franco-Allemand pour la Jeunesse.* Frankfurt: DIPF

Barley, N. 1990 *Native Land.* Harmondsworth: Penguin Books

Barr, A. and York, P. 1982 *The Official Sloane Ranger Handbook.* London: Ebury Press

Baumgratz, G., and Stephan, R. 1987 *Fremdsprachenlernen als Beitrag zur internationalen Verständigung. Inhaltliche und organisatorische Perspektiven der Lehrerfortbildung in Europa.* München: iudicium

Baumgratz-Gangl, G. and Deyson, N. 1990 *Mobility of Students in Europe: Linguistic and Socio-cultural Conditions.* (A study carried out for the Commission of the European Communities) Brussels/Luxembourg

Beneke, J. (ed.) 1993a *Arbeitspapiere zur Internationalen Unternehmenskommunikation.* Communication in Aviation Series. Bonn: Dümmler Verlag

Beneke, J. 1993b 'English as the Medium of Intercultural Communication: Some Teaching Suggestions'. In Beneke 1993a

Bergentoft, R. 1987 *Consolidated Report on the School Interaction Network.* Strasbourg: Council of Europe Press

Bergentoft, R. 1989 'Learning and Teaching Languages in European Schools: The Interaction School Network of Project 12'. In Council of Europe 1989

Best, Y. de 1994 'Opvoeden in Nederland. Hoe doen we het Eigenlijk?'. In *Ouders van Nu*, May 1994 pp39ff. Haarlem: Spaarnestad BV

Bliss, I. 1990 'Intercultural Education and the Professional Knowledge of Teachers'. In *European Journal of Teacher Education* vol.13, no.3

Blundell, J. 1984 *English Visa.* Oxford: Oxford University Press

Bouwens, F. en Oud-de Glas, M. 1991 bespreking van *Het vreemdetalenonderwijs in de onderbouw van het voortgezet onderwijs.* Amsterdam/Lisse: Swets & Zeitlinger BV. (A review of this study, entitled 'Engels, Duits en Frans in onderbouw voorgezet onderwijs'. In *Didaktief*, Dec. 1990.

Bouwens, F. en Oud-de Glas, M. 1991 *Het vreemdetalen onderwijs in de onderbouw van het voortgezet onderwijs.* Amsterdam/Lisse: Swets and Zeitlinger BV

Breen, M. 1985 'The Social Context for Language Learning – A Neglected Situation?'. In *Studies in Second Language Acquisition* vol.7, pp135–58

Brookes, A. and Grundy, P. 1988 *Individualization and Autonomy in Language Learning.* ELT Documents 131. London: Modern English Publications in association with the British Council

Brown, H. D. 1987 *Principles of Language Learning and Teaching*, second edition. Englewood Cliffs, N.J.: Prentice Hall

Buford, B. 1992 *Among the Thugs.* London: Mandarin Paperbacks

Byram, M. 1992 'Foreign Language Learning for European Citizenship'. In *Language Learning Journal* no.6

Byram, M. and Esarte-Sarries, V. 1991 *Investigating Cultural Studies in Foreign Language Teaching.* Clevedon, Avon/Philadelphia: Multilingual Matters

Byram, M., Morgan, C. and Colleagues 1994 *Teaching and Learning Language and Culture.* Clevedon, Avon/Philadelphia/Adelaide: Multilingual Matters

Calvin, W. H. 1986 *The River that Flows Uphill.* San Francisco: Sierra Club Books

Campbell, C. and Kryszewska, H. 1992 *Learner-based Teaching.* Oxford: Oxford University Press

Candlin, C. (ed.) 1981 *The Communicative Teaching of English, Principles and an Exercise Typology.* London: Longman

Candlin, C. and Edelhoff, C. (eds.) 1989 *Verstehen und Verständigung. Festschrift für Hans-Eberhard Piepho.* Bochum: Kamp

Candlin, E. F. 1972 *New Present Day English for Foreign Students.* London: Hodder and Stoughton

Carroll, R. 1988 *Cultural Misunderstandings.* The French American Experience. Chicago: The University of Chicago Press

Chang, J. 1991 *Wild Swans.* London: Flamingo, HarperCollins Publishers

Chomsky, N. 1959 'A Review of B. F. Skinner's: *Verbal Behavior*'. In *Language* vol.35, pp26–58

Chomsky, N. 1965 *Aspects of the Theory of Syntax.* Cambridge, Mass.: The MIT Press

Christophersen, P. 1973 *Second-Language Learning.* Harmondsworth: Penguin

Cornford, A., Bosschaart, G., van Daalen, K., Hordijk, H., Lincklaen Arriëns, M. and Spuy, G. 1994 *Interface*, Coursebook 1. Amsterdam: Meulenhoff Educatief

Council of Europe 1973 *Systems Development in Adult Language Learning.* Strasbourg: Council of Europe Press

Council of Europe 1984 *Self-assessment of Foreign Language Skills: A Survey of Research and Development Work.* Strasbourg: Council of Europe Press

Council of Europe 1988 *Evaluation and Testing in the Learning and Teaching of Languages for Communication.* Strasbourg: Council of Europe Press

Council of Europe 1989 *Conference: Language Learning in Europe: The Challenge of Diversity.* Strasbourg: Council of Europe Press

Crichton, M. 1969 *A Case of Need.* New York: Signet Books, Penguin Books USA, Inc

Crystal, D. 1988 *The English Language.* Harmondsworth: Pelican Books, Penguin Books

Dekker, H. en Deckers J. 1992 *Internationalisering van hoger onderwijs.* Utrecht: VSNU

Duda, R. and Riley, P. 1990 *Learning Styles.* Nancy: Presses Universitaires de Nancy

Edelhoff, C. (ed.) 1978 *Kommunikativer Englischunterricht, Prinzipien und Übungstypologie.* Bundesarbeitsgemeinschaft Englisch an Gesamtschulen, München: Langenscheidt-Longman

Edelhoff, C. 1984 'Landeskunde zum Anfassen – The Lancaster Outing'. In Schratz

Edelhoff, C. 1987 '"Landeskunde" Requirements for Foreign Language Teachers'. In Baumgratz and Stephan

Ellis, G. and Sinclair, B. 1989 *Learning to Learn English*, Teacher's Book, Learner's Book. Cambridge: Cambridge University Press

Ellis, W. 1994 *The Oxbridge Conspiracy. How the Ancient Universities Have Kept their Stranglehold on the Establishment.* London: Michael Joseph

Erp, A. J. M. van 1991 *The Phonetic Basis of Personality Ratings*. Voorburg: PTT Research

Fairclough, N. 1989 *Language and Power*. Harlow: Longman

Faerch, C., Haastrup, K. and Phillipson, R. 1984 *Learner Language and Language Learning*. Clevedon, Avon: Multilingual Matters

Frank, C. and Rinvolucri, M. 1987 *Grammar in Action Again*. Pilgrims. London: Prentice-Hall International (UK)

Galjee, W. (ed.) 1989 *Proposals for National Criteria Modern Languages in the First Phase of Secondary Education: General Objectives and Concrete Core Objectives*. Enschede: SLO (Foundation for Curriculum Development)

Gardner, R. C. and Lambert, W. E. 1972 *Attitudes and Motivation in Second-Language Learning*. Rowley, Mass.: Newbury House Publishers

Glade-Hasenmüller, H. n.d. *Zeg's Scheveningen!*. Velp: HPP Hassenmüller Publication/Amsterdam: Uitgeverij Gigant

Gray, K. 1990 'Syllabus Design for the General Class: What Happens to Theory When you Apply it'. In *English Language Teaching Journal* Vol.44, no.4

Green, P. S. (ed.) 1987 *Communicative Language Testing, A Resource Handbook for Teacher Trainers*. Strasbourg: Council of Europe Press

Gumperz, J. J. 1982 *Discourse Strategies*. Cambridge: Cambridge University Press

Hagendoorn, L. and Linssen, H. 1991 'Nationale karakteristieken en stereotypen'. Algemene Sociale Wetenschappen, Rijksuniversiteit Utrecht, Postbus 80140, 3508 TC Utrecht, photocopy

Harrison, B. (ed.) 1990 *Culture and the Language Classroom*. ELT Documents. London: Modern English Publications in association with the British Council

Hatch, E. 1983 *Psycholinguistics: A Second Language Perspective*. Rowley, Mass.: Newbury House Publishers

Hatch, E. 1992 *Discourse and Language Education*. Cambridge: Cambridge University Press

Haugen, E. 1973 'The Stigmata of Bilingualism'. In Pride

Havranek, G. and Stefan, F. 1990 *Fremdsprachendidaktik und Innovation in der Lehrerbildung*. Wien: Böhlau Verlag

Herbert, F. with Herbert, B. 1987 *Man of Two Worlds*. New York: Ace Books

Hilgard, E. R., Atkinson, R. C. and Atkinson, R. L. 1971 *Introduction to Psychology*, fifth edition. San Diego, Calif.: Harcourt Brace Jovanovich Inc.

Hill, R. 1992 *We Europeans*. Brussels: Europublications

Hofstede, G. 1991 *Cultures and Organizations: Software of the Mind*. London: McGraw Hill

Hofstede, G. 1993 *Images of Europe*, Valedictory address on the occasion of his retirement as a professor of Organizational Anthropology and International Management, Maastricht

Holec, H. 1980 *Autonomy and Foreign Language Learning*. Strasbourg: Council of Europe Press

Holec, H. 1988 *Autonomy and Self-directed Learning: Present Fields of Application*. Strasbourg: Council of Europe Press

Hymes, D. 1972 'On communicative Competence'. In Pride and Holmes

Jackendoff, R. 1993 *Patterns in the Mind*. Language and Human Nature. Hemel Hempstead: Harvester Wheatsheaf

Jong, W. N. de 1989 'The Language Teaching Profession: In a State of Flux?'. In *European Journal of Teacher Education*, vol.12, no.2, pp169–77

Jong, W. N. de 1993 'Training EFL-Teachers for Multicultural Schools'. In *The Teacher Trainer*, vol.7, no.2, pp14–16

Jong, W. N. de 1996 'English, its Place in Learning about Other Cultures: A Plea for Learner-autonomy in the English Language Classroom as a Requirement for the Development of Socio-Cultural Competence'. In Willems 1996

Jong, W. de en Willems, G. M. 1992 'Transculturele gespreksvaardigheid; taalvaardigheid in internationalisering van onderwijs'. In Dekker en Deckers

Kachru, B. B. 1986 *The Alchemy of English: The Spread, Functions and Models of Non-native Englishes*. Oxford: Pergamon Press

Kasper, G. (ed.) 1986 *Learning, Teaching and Communication in the Foreign Language Classroom*. Aarhus: Aarhus University Press

Kellerman, E. J. 1987 *Aspects of Transferability in Second Language Acquisition*. Enschede: Sneldruk

Kellerman, E. J. and Sharwood Smith, M. (eds.) 1986 *Crosslinguistic Influences in Second Language Acquisition*. Oxford: Pergamon Press

Klippel, F. 1984 *Keep Talking*. Cambridge: Cambridge University Press

Kohonen, V. *et al.* 1988 *Evaluation and Testing in the Learning and Teaching of Languages for Communication*. Strasbourg: Council of Europe Press

Kramsch, C. 1993 *Context and Culture in Language Teaching*. Oxford: Oxford University Press

Kramsch, C. 1993 'Language Study as Border Study: Experiencing Difference'. In *European Journal of Education* vol.28, no.3

Larsen-Freeman, D. and Long, M. H. 1991 *An Introduction to Second Language Acquisition Research*. Harlow: Longman

Legutke, M. and Thomas, H. 1991 *Process and Experience in the Language Classroom*. Harlow: Longman

Little, D. 1991 *Learner Autonomy*. Dublin: Authentik Language Learning Resources

Littlewood, W. 1992 *Teaching Oral Communication*. Oxford: Blackwell

Luukas, A. and Nordlund, J. 1994 *Challenge, English for Communication*. Otava: Helsingissä Kustannusosakeyhtiö

Lyons, J. 1981 *Language and Linguistics*. Cambridge: Cambridge University Press

Maley, A. and Duff, A. 1982 *Drama Techniques in Language Learning*, second edition. Cambridge: Cambridge University Press

McCarthy, M. 1991 *Discourse Analysis for Language Teachers*. Cambridge: Cambridge University Press

McCarthy, M. and Carter, R. 1993 *Language as Discourse: Perspectives for Language Teaching*. Harlow: Longman

McCrum, R., Cran, W. and McNeil, R. 1986 *The Story of English*. London: Faber & Faber and BBC Publications

Mead, M. 1963 *Coming of Age in Samoa*. Harmondsworth: Penguin Books

Miedema, R. (ed.) 1989 *Voices After the Conference. European Voices on Quality, Personality and Methodology.* Report on the 7th international workshop, Zeist

Ministerie van Onderwijs en Wetenschappen 1968 *Voorstel Leerplan rijksscholen voor vwo/havo/mavo.* Den Haag: author

Ministerie van Onderwijs en Wetenschappen 1989 *Advies over de voorlopige eindtermen in de basisvorming van het voortgezet onderwijs. Moderne Vreemde Talen.* Zoetermeer: author

Morris, D. 1977 *Manwatching.* London: Jonathan Cape

Naipaul, V. S. 1969 *The Suffrage of Elvira.* Harmondsworth: Penguin Books

Nemetz Robinson, G. (ed.) 1985 *Crosscultural Understanding.* Oxford: Pergamon Press

Neuner, G. 1988 *A Socio-cultural Framework for Communicative Teaching and Learning of Foreign Languages at the School Level.* Strasbourg: Council of Europe Press

Neuner, G., Krüger, M. and Grewer, U. 1981 *Übungstypologie zum kommunikativen Deutschunterricht.* München: Langenscheidt

Nolasco, R. and Arthur, L. 1987 *Conversation.* Oxford: Oxford University Press

Norman, D., Levihn, U. and Hedenquist, J. A. 1986 *Communicative Ideas.* Hove: Language Teaching Publications

Nunan, D. 1989 *Designing Tasks for the Communicative Classroom.* Cambridge: Cambridge University Press

Nunan, D. 1991 *Language Teaching Methodology.* Hemel Hempstead: Prentice Hall International

Nunan, D. (ed.) 1992 *Collaborative Language Learning and Teaching.* Cambridge: Cambridge University Press

O'Neill, R. 1987 *Success at First Certificate.* Oxford: Oxford University Press

Oskarsson, M. 1978 *Approaches to Self-assessment in Foreign Language Learning.* Oxford: Pergamon Press

Pattison, P. 1987 *Developing Communication Skills.* Cambridge: Cambridge University Press

Pattison, P. 1989 'Pupil Motivation and Oral Communication Skills'. In Willems and Riley 1989

Phillipson, R. 1992 *Linguistic Imperialism.* Oxford: Oxford University Press

Pinker, S. 1994 *The Language Instinct.* London: Penguin Books

Platt, J., Weber, H. and Ho, M. L. 1984 *The New Englishes.* London: Routledge and Kegan Paul

Porcher, L. 1980 *Reflections on Language Needs in the School.* Strasbourg: Council of Europe Press

Preston, D. R. and Shuy, R. W. 1984 *Varieties of American English. A Reader.* Washington: USIS

Pride, J. B. (ed.) 1979 *Sociolinguistic Aspects of Language Learning and Teaching.* Oxford: Oxford University Press

Pride, J. B. and Holmes, J. (eds.) 1972 *Sociolinguistics.* Harmondsworth: Penguin Books

Pruitt, D. G. and Carnevale, P. 1993 *Negotiation in Social Conflict.* Buckingham: Open University Press

Quirk, R. and Widdowson, H. G. (eds.) 1985 *English in the World: Teaching and Learning the Language and Literatures.* Cambridge: Cambridge University Press

Renier, G. J. 1931/1956 *The English: Are they Human?* fourth edition. Ernest Benn

Rey, M. 1986 *Training Teachers in Intercultural Education?.* Strasbourg: Council of Europe Press

Richards, J. 1972 'Social Factors, Interlanguage and Language Learning'. In Pride

Riley, P. 1984 'Your Slip is Showing: Communicative Interference in Second Language Learning'. In Willems and Riley 1984

Riley, P. (ed.) 1985 *Discourse and Learning.* Harlow: Longman

Riley, P. 1989a 'There's Nothing as Practical as a Good Theory': Research, Teaching and Learning Functions of Language Centres. In *Mélanges Pédagogiques*, pp73–87. Nancy: CRAPEL

Riley, P. 1989b 'Social Identity and Intercultural Communication'. In *Levende Talen*, 443, pp488–93

Riley, P. 1989c 'Keeping Secrets: ESP/LSP and the Sociology of Knowledge'. In *European Journal of Teacher Education*, vol.12, no.2, pp69–81

Rinvolucri, M. 1984 *Grammar Games.* Cambridge: Cambridge University Press

Rivers, W. 1968 *Teaching Foreign-Language Skills* p39. Chicago: University of Chicago Press

Rönnqvist, L. and Sell, R. D. 1994 'Teenage Books for Teenagers: Reflections on Literature in Language Education'. In *English Language Teaching Journal* vol.48, no.2

Rutherford, W. 1987 *Second Language Grammar: Learning and Teaching.* Harlow: Longman

Rutten, H. and Van Ruyssevelt, F. 1986 *Notting Hill Gate.* 's Hertogenbosch: Malmberg

Sampson, A. 1984 *The Changing Anatomy of Britain.* London: Vintage Books

Sampson, A. 1989 *The Midas Touch.* Sevenoaks: Coronet Books

Saville-Troike, M. 1982 *The Ethnography of Communication.* Oxford: Blackwell

Scarcella, R. 1990 *Teaching Language Minority Students in the Multilingual Classroom.* Englewood Cliffs, N.J.: Prentice Hall

Schratz, M. (ed.) 1984 *Englischunterricht im Gespräch.* Bochum: Kamp

Shapiro, R. 1986 *Origins: A Sceptic's Guide to the Creation of Life on Earth.* London: Heinemann

Sheerin, S. 1989 *Self-access.* Oxford: Oxford University Press

Sheils, J. 1988 *Communication in the Modern Languages Classroom.* Strasbourg: Council of Europe Press

Sinclair, J. McH. and Coulthard, R. M. 1975 *Towards an Analysis of Discourse: The English Used by Teachers and Pupils.* Oxford: Oxford University Press

Smith, L. E. (ed.) 1987 *Discourse across Cultures.* Hemel Hempstead: Prentice Hall International

Stern, H. H. 1983 *Fundamental Concepts of Language Teaching*, Oxford: Oxford University Press

Stern, H. H. 1992 *Issues and Options in Language Teaching.* Oxford: Oxford University Press

Strange, J. *et al.* 1994 *Friends, International English.* Houten: Educaboek

Tarone, E. 1988 *Variation in Interlanguage.* London: Edward Arnold

Theroux, P. 1983 *The Mosquito Coast.* Harmondsworth: Penguin Books

Tomalin, B. and Stempleski, S. 1993 *Cultural Awareness.* Oxford: Oxford University Press

Trim, J. L. M. (general rapporteur) 1985 *Symposium on the Initial and In-service Training of Teachers of Modern Languages.* Strasbourg: Council of Europe Press

Trudgill, P. and Hannah, J. 1982 *International English: A Guide to Varieties of Standard English.* London: Edward Arnold

Ur, P. 1981 *Discussions that Work*. Cambridge: Cambridge University Press

Ur, P. 1988 *Grammar Practice Activities*. Cambridge: Cambridge University Press

Valdes, J. M. (ed.) 1986 *Culture Bound. Bridging the Cultural Gap in Language Teaching*. Cambridge: Cambridge University Press

Van Dijck, H. (ed.) 1991 *Europe for Everybody. Texts on European Integration*. Nijmegen: Hogeschool Gelderland

van Ek, J. A. 1975 *The Threshold Level*. Strasbourg: Council of Europe Press

van Ek, J. A. 1976 *The Threshold Level for Modern Language Learning in Schools*. Groningen: Wolters-Noordhoff-Longman

van Ek, J. A. 1986 *Objectives for Foreign Language Learning. Volume 1: Scope*. Strasbourg: Council of Europe Press

van Ek, J. A. 1987 *Objectives for Foreign Language Learning. Volume 2: Levels*. Strasbourg: Council of Europe Press

van Ek, J. A., Alexander, L. G. and Fitzpatrick, M. A. 1977 *Waystage English*. Oxford: Pergamon Press

van Ek, J. A. and Trim, J. L. M. 1991 *The Threshold Level, Version 1990*. Strasbourg: Council of Europe Press

van Els, T., Bongaerts, T., Extra, G., van Os, C. and Janssen-van Dieten, A.-M. 1984 *Applied Linguistics and the Learning and Teaching of Foreign Languages*. London: Edward Arnold

van Essen, A. J. 1989a 'Grammar: Its Place in Foreign-Language Education'. In *Der Fremdsprachlichen Unterricht*. 23/96, pp4–10, Kam Verlag

van Essen, A. J. 1989b 'The Continental European Contribution to EFL, Past and Present'. In Candlin and Edelhoff

van Essen, A. J. 1991 'English Among the Other European Languages'. In *English – a World Language* vol.1, no.2, pp6–13

Wajnryb, R. 1990 *Grammar Dictation*. Oxford: Oxford University Press

Waters, A., Sunderland, J., Bray, T. and Allwright, J. 1990 'Getting the Best out of "The Language-learning Experience"'. In *English Language Teaching Journal* vol.44, no.4

Wetering, J. W. van de 1978 *The Corpse on the Dike*. New York: Pocket Books

Widdicombe, S. and Wooffitt, R. 1995 *The Language of Youth Subcultures*. Hemel Hempstead: Harvester Wheatsheaf

Widdowson, H. G. 1987 *A Rationale for Language Teacher Education*. Strasbourg: Council of Europe Press

Widdowson, H. G. 1991 *Aspects of Language Teaching*. Oxford: Oxford University Press

Wilkins, D. 1987 *The Educational Value of Foreign Language Learning*. Strasbourg: Council of Europe Press

Willems, G. M. 1990 'Foreign Languages for Communication. Some New Perspectives'. In Havranek and Stefan

Willems, G. M. 1991 'Transcultural Communicative Competence and the Growth of European Citizenship'. In Van Dijck

Willems, G. M. 1993a 'Oral Foreign Language Use; an Exercise in Cross-cultural Strategic Behaviour'. In Beneke 1993a

Willems, G. M. 1993b (ed.) *Attainment Targets for Foreign Language Teacher Education in Europe*. ATEE Cahiers No.5, Association of Teacher Education in Europe, 60 Rue de la Concorde, B 1050-Brussels

Willems, G. M. (ed.) 1994 *The Introduction of the European Dimension in Education. The Role of Foreign Language Teaching*. Project of Sub-Network No. 9 of the Network of Teacher Education Institutes, Nijmegen: Hogeschool Gelderland Pers

Willems, G. M. 1996a 'Culture in Language Learning and Teaching; Requirements for the Creation of a Context of Negotiation'. In Willems 1996b

Willems, G. (ed.) 1996b *Issues in Cross-cultural Communication; Lessons for Language Teaching*. Nijmegen: Hogeschool Gelderland Pers

Willems, G. M. and Jong, W. N. de 1989 'Foreign Language Command: Definition and Description'. In *European Journal of Teacher Education* vol.12, no.2, pp81–97

Willems, G. M. and Riley, P. (eds.) 1984 *Communicative Foreign Language Teaching and the Training of Foreign Language Teachers*. Nijmegen: Interstudie Institute for Teacher Education

Willems, G. M. and Riley, P. (eds.) 1989 *Foreign Language Learning and Teaching in Europe*. Amsterdam: Bureau Lerarenopleiding and Free University Press

Wong, R. 1985 'Does Pronunciation Teaching Have a Place in the Communicative Classroom?' In *Proceedings of Georgetown Round Table on Languages and Linguistics*. Washington, D. C.: Georgetown University Press

Wright, A., Betteridge, D. and Buckby, M. 1979. *Games for Language Learning*. Cambridge: Cambridge University Press

Dictionaries and Journals

Longman Dictionary of Contemporary English third edition. Harlow and London: Longman

Longman Dictionary of English Language and Culture 1992. Harlow: Longman

Partridge, E. 1978 *Origins. A Short Etymological Dictionary of Modern English*. Book Club Associates

Shorter Oxford English Dictionary 1966 third edition. Oxford: Oxford University Press

World Englishes. Journal of English as an International and Transnational Language. Oxford: Pergamon Press